INDRA

FIRST OF THE ARYAS

INDRA
FIRST OF THE ARYAS

ABHIVEER

NU VOICE PRESS

NU VOICE PRESS

First published by NU VOICE PRESS 2023
An imprint of Hubhawks Pvt. Ltd
www.nuvoicepress.com

This is a work of fiction and all characters and incidents described in this book are the product of the author's imagination. Any resemblance to actual persons, living or dead, is entirely coincidental.

ISBN: 978-81-963184-9-9

Typeset by Saanvi Graphics, Noida
Printed at Thomson Press
Published by Nu Voice Press

For Pari;

The one who forced me to take breaks and play both while doing homework and writing this book.

AUTHOR'S NOTE

From my childhood, Indra was my favourite Deva. Cartoons, Movies, Puranic stories and Daily Soaps often showed him in a misogynistic, comical and antagonistic point of view that the Vedic myths of his bravery are hidden away. But I always seemed to have a soft corner and a deep admiration for him. He's the only Rigvedic deity that appears the most human.

A discussion in my family often turned into a heated argument with me ranting about Indra's "heroic" side.

Often, in the summer heat of my classroom, my classmates would hope for a shower to cool the Earth.

Three hours into the book and, it began to rain in May! Was it a sign from the gods? No idea. But the monsoon has always remained and will continue to remain my favourite season. The rains are the best.

This book is a tribute to my favourite god, Lord Indra, the God of Rain and Thunder.

CHARACTER LIST

Adinath- Aghori from Kashi, Bhairav's disciple

Airavata- Indra's albino elephant.

Ambika- Pashupati's wife

Anha- Kalakeya treasurer

Anshuman- Aditya (Deva military rank)

Arbuda- Kalakeya warrior, Guardian of the Fiery Sky-Lingam Temple of Shiva and assistant to Shukracharya

Arun- Mohenjo-Daro's strongest wrestler

Aryaman- Deva General

Bhaga- Deva treasurer

Bhairav- The Rudra, representative of Lord Shiva

Bhrigu of the Angiras

Brihaspati- Guru of Mitra-Varuna and Indra, the Chief of the Angiras

Chandan- Asura Chief Minister

Chandra- Former King of Mohenjo-Daro

Dadhyanch- mysterious Brahmin from the Angiras

Danu- Vritra's mother

Dasra- Nasatya's twin, an excellent swordsman

Dharma- General of the Nagas

Dyaus- King of the Devas and Prajapatis, Fifth head of Brahma.

Hiranyastupa- Brihaspati's successor as Chief of the Angiras

Indra- The Devendra, king of the Devas and successor to Dyaus

Jayant- Indra's son

Jayanti- Indra's daughter and Jayant's twin. Named after Deva noblewoman who lived many centuries ago

Kshetrapaal- Former Rudra, Bhairav's predecessor

Kutsa- assistant to Hiranyastupa

Markandeya- Bhairav's disciple

Martand- Commander of the Maruts

Matarishvan- Marut

Mitra- Indra's elder brother, titled as 'Ahura' after Slaying of the Bull

Nasatya- Indra's adopted brother, an excellent horseman

Parnaya and Karanja- Vangrida's sons

Parvata- Chief of the Panis

Pashupati- Bhairav's successor as Rudra

Pipru- Servant in Lakhanjo-Daro

Prithvi- Dyaus' wife

Pushan- Deva Police Chief

Ribhu, Vibhu and Vaja- Craftsmen Angira brothers

Rijishva- Former King of Indraprastha, Pashupati's General, also called Divodas and Athithigva

Rodasi- Commander of the Maruts, Indra's bodyguards

Sarama- Indra's pet bitch

Sargon the Great- First ruler of the Akkadian Empire

Savitar- Father of Nasatya and Dasra

Shambara- General of Lakhanjo-Daro

Sharvar and Shyam- Indra's pups

Shushna- Vritra's general.

Sunetra- Vangrida's first wife

Suviryavan- King of the Pataal Nivatakavachas

Takshak III- The Nagaraja, King of the Nagas

Tara- Wife of Brihaspati

Tarakaksh, **Kamalaksh** and **Vidyunmali**- Governors of Tripura

Turvasu- Chief of Staff of Vangrida's palace

Tvashtri- Angira craftsman

Urvashi- Mitra's wife and Vashishth's mother

Vangrida- Fort commander of Lakhanjo Daro

Varuna- Mitra's twin brother

Vashishth Maitravaruni- Mitra's son

Vichitra- Chief of the Northern Kalakeyas

Virupaksh- Bhairav's Dhaman

Vrishabh- Marut soldier

Vrishakapi- Chief of the Persian Vaanars

Vritra- Assyrian warlord and Right-hand man of the Emperor, Unifier of the Kalakeyas

TRIBES AND CLANS

Angiras- The tribe of Lord Agni, the god of fire

Apsaras- A tribe of wandering courtesans, they are often likened to water nymphs due to their sensuous water dances.

Asuras- The Asuras are an ancient tribe. Literally translated as 'Lords,' they have always been the poorer and weaker tribe. They are divided into-

Bhutaganas- The tribe of the Rudra, the representative of Lord Shiva

Chandravanshis- Descendants of the Moon god, most populous non-Asura tribe.

- **Daityas-** The Daityas are further divided into Kalakeyas and Nivatakavachas and a few minor clans
- **Danavas**

Devas- Once revered as Gods, the Devas now live as outcasts in the desert of Bactria. Their society is divided into four castes or Varnas. They are the Brahmins, priests teachers, and doctors; the Kshatriyas, warriors and aristocracy; the Vaishyas who are the traders and merchants and the Shudras, the menial workers. The system of caste division is partly birth-based and partly occupation and skills/education-based.

They are democratic but the Kings are elected only from the previous King's family

Gandharvas- A northern tribe who excel in archery, horse warfare, music, and other forms of art

Garudas- Arch-enemies of the Nagas, their emblem is an eagle and they worship Lord Vishnu. Some time ago, they possessed the now-lost technology of Vimanas, flying machines.

Nagas- A serpent-worshipping tribe. They revere Lord Shiva, natural elements, animals, poisonous plants, and their old chiefs who are deified. They are democratic during peacetime and dictatorial during wartime

Panis- An Asura clan that likes to hoard, trade and pillage

Prajapatis- The tribe of Lord Brahma

Rakshasas- A martial clan from the South of Aryavarta, they are bitter enemies of the Vaanars

Suryavanshis- Descendants of the Sun God, second-most populous non-Asura tribe of the Sapta-Sindhu

Vaanars- The Vaanars resemble monkeys. A mutation makes them look like apes with disfigured, protruding jaws, extra fingers, and even tails.

Yakshas- A tribe composed almost entirely of traders

MILITARY RANKS, NAMES AND TITLES

Aditya- Deva commander

Agastya- Highest-ranking Brahmin in southern Aryavarta

Ahura- Lord, Noble

Ashwin- Deva cavalry commander

Avatar of Vishnu- representative of Lord Vishnu

Bhutapati- the Rudra's lieutenant

Brahmin- Priests, doctors and teachers, the Brahmins refer to the occupationally intellectual. They are the top Varna of the society

Devendra- King of the Devas

Firstborn of the Dragons- Vritra's official designation

Fort Commander- Fort governor of the Kalakeyas

Head of Brahma- representative of Lord Brahma

Kshatriya- Warriors and soldiers, they form the second layer of society

Maruts- Deva emergency soldiers

Mleccha- outsiders, foreigners, barbarians

Nagaraja- Chief General or King of the Nagas

Raudras- the Rudra's personal bodyguards

Rudra- the representative of Lord Shiva

Saptarishi- A group of seven Brahmins who are supposed to guard the ancient knowledge

Shudra- do menial jobs and serve the above three classes. Propaganda suggests that the Devas mistreat those who are "born-low," but in fact, only a tiny portion of the Shudras are born so

Shukracharya- Head priest of the Kalakeyas

Unifier of the Kalakeyas- Vritra's epithet

Vaishya- moneymakers like merchants, businessmen and traders

I now declare the laudable deeds of Indra, the first that he achieved, the Thunder-wielder.

He slew the Dragon, then disclosed the waters, and cleft the channels of the mountain torrents.

He slew the Dragon lying on the mountain: his heavenly bolt of thunder Tvashtri fashioned.

Like lowing kine in rapid flow descending the waters glided downward to the ocean.

Impetuous as a bull, he chose the Soma and in three sacred beakers drank the juices.

The Great One grasped the thunder for his weapon, and smote to death this firstborn of the dragons.

–Rig Veda, 1.32

PROLOGUE

1800 BCE, at the banks of the Saraswati River

The man was trying to meditate under the tree. But the young children just couldn't let him concentrate. From their looks and conduct, they seem to be in their early twenties.

"Deserved it, that bastard," one said.

"That rascal turned green right in the first punch," a boy with a deeper complexion smirked.

Descendants of the gods, they call them, he thought to himself.

"*Oye*, kids!" someone yelled.

"Yes, Grandpa," the dusky one responded, and the rest howled with laughter.

Ignoring everyone, the old man continued, "The river that flows where you're playing is sacred. She is the mother of our civilisation in Aryavarta. You cannot use expletives near her."

The oldest of the lot of children replied, "Or what? I shall curse the river, too! May it f—"

What happened next was so quick that the boy had little to no time to react. The old man's cane struck the boy's skull, and an audible crack was heard. The boy fell down into the holy waters of the Saraswati. The old man lowered his stick in the river to help the youth on his feet.

Everyone stared at the old man. He was clad in a white *dhoti.* He looked more than eighty years of age. His hands looked frail and wrinkled. Nearly bald with a leathery egg-shaped head, he had thin wisps coming out. He donned a silver beard with his weak physical demeanour. His ribs were clearly visible, and it seemed that they might shatter into pieces if he tried to pick up the heavy book next to the tree he was sitting under. His bloodshot eyes and cracked teeth added to the general air of unpleasantness surrounding him. Clearly, he was no warrior. Yet, the hit on the boy's head drew out a pool of blood.

"For Lord Agni's sake, take away this twit and get him to see a medicine man now," he said to the boys, who stood stunned.

"Wh-Who…Who are you?" one of the boys asked.

The man groaned. He was bound by the laws of his tribe to never speak a lie as they were supposed to be knowledge-givers; mediators between the gods and men. This also meant that he would have to leave the place and settle somewhere else as per the laws.

"I can't lie to you. Have you heard of the Angira tribe?"

The boys stared with shock. The Angiras were the famous tribe used by Lord Indra—the King of the Devas—for reconnaissance a few centuries ago. However, they were the subject of bedtime stories and not actual groups of people. At least, they used to be, till a few centuries ago. But demons don't exist. And neither do Warrior Sages, who claim their descent from the Fire God—Lord Agni.

"Woah. You mean you…you…"

To add to everyone's shock, the old man nodded.

"Then it means that the... the Devas...Indra...Lord... In..."

He nodded again

"But then it means...Demons... Vritra..."

"Would you like to hear a story?" the old man asked.

Everyone was confused as they looked at their injured companion and then at the old man.

"Take him to a doctor and meet me here in the evening. Though I have to leave today now since... anyways, a few hours won't matter."

The boys grabbed their injured comrade and moved towards the town.

1

The Bactrian Steppe, 2300 BCE

The rider wiped the sweat beads off his forehead. The Bactrian sun burned his back as the horse moved along the steppe. If one looked outside a window, one would think that it was a desert, which was true. Bactria, indeed, was a desert. An extremely cold one.

The numerous layers of shawls and jackets worn by the people were enough to attest to the level of the cold.

The rider had an unclean, dishevelled look as if he hadn't bathed for many days. His black, full beard, barrel chest, and pot belly indicated that he was in his mid-forties. In reality, he was over eighty. Nervously fidgeting, he turned and looked towards the hill. An attack was expected.

Maybe I have left them far behind, he thought.

As he contemplated stopping and resting, a loud conch was blown. The rider instantly recognised the conch.

From the top of the hill came a trident-shaped arrow. It whizzed by his ear and landed near the foot of his horse. It was enough to kick the animal into action. The horse bolted, without its rider, into the wilderness. The man fell on his back into the sand.

A group of ten riders descended from the hill. They were carrying a flag that had a picture of a bull. It was the flag of the Bhutaganas.

The common belief amongst the people of Sapta-Sindhu—Land of the Seven Rivers, i.e., India— was that the Universe was maintained by the Trinity, a group of three gods—the Creator, the Preserver and the Destroyer. These were Lord Brahma, Lord Vishnu and Lord Shiva, respectively. They all had human representatives on Earth with interconnected roles.

The civilisation, which had become so decadent that it deserved destruction, had to be destroyed. This was Lord Shiva's task. Lord Brahma's task was to create a new way of life, and it was Lord Narayana's task to preserve the new way of life.

Everyone thought there was only one Lord Brahma. However, there were four Great Brahmas, or 'four heads of Brahma', as they were called since ages. The fifth lay in the Bactrian sand.

The man tried to make a run for his life.

A loud whoosh, a stabbing noise and a crack echoed. A spear pierced the femur bone in his thigh.

"You can't run away this time, you sneaky son of a two-headed jackal," someone shouted.

The fallen rider groaned with exasperation. He recognised the voice, and he hated it. It was none other than the 'Rudra', the leader of the Bhutaganas. Rudra was a title passed down from one Bhutagana leader to another. The devout followers maintained that a Rudra was the human representative of Lord Shiva on Earth.

The current Rudra, Bhairav, was a sadistic man. He liked to eat raw flesh. He wore skulls and bones as a garland and smeared ash from crematoriums on his body. His black dhoti was tied tight on his waist with a dead snake. A black hound tied to a leash was desperately trying to free itself to attack the fallen man.

"Bhairav! What an honour to see you!" the man said, trying to sound as cheerful as possible.

"It's Lord Rudra, you scum!"

The impatient dog growled and tried to lunge at the rider.

"You dare steal from the ancient vaults of—" The Rudra saw an empty satchel on the sand.

"Oh, Hell no! Lord Shiva, have mercy! You scoundrel, where is it? WHERE IS IT, YOU BASTARD!?"

The man smiled as he was well aware of the Rudra's temper.

Bhairav drew out his sword from the scabbard. The markings on the blade were familiar to the man. It was an ancient script from the lands of the Sindhu and Saraswati. It was a simple inscription of *Chandrahaas.*

"Kill me. But I will not tell you anything."

Bhairav drew in a deep breath, "You don't deserve your title as the Fifth head of Brahma, Dyaus," the Rudra stabbed the man in the gut. His rage knew no bounds. He hacked at the body even after the man died and beheaded the corpse.

"SPREAD OUT AND SEARCH FOR IT!"

The hound sniffed the body and followed his master.

2

"What?" Prithvi was shocked. Her husband, Dyaus, had vanished in the desert. His horse had been found the previous night in the desert. Dead. Its carcass being feasted upon by vultures. The soldiers recognised it because of the royal seal marked on the saddle—the royal seal of the Devas.

There used to be a time when the Devas were looked upon as gods in the Sapta-Sindhu. However, after the Kurukshetra War, things changed rapidly. After a few centuries, the Asuras who had been hiding came out. Since there was a shortage of men, the Devas could not fight and were forced into exile.

The Deva Empire, Amaravati, had its capital as New Amaravati. The towering bastions, thick walls and proud banners were a picture of majesty. The city was established by Lord Meghavahan, the King of the Devas, during the Kurukshetra war.

The Bactrian Plain was one place where the Devas could live in peace. Along with them came other tribes terrorised by the Asuras, such as the Gandharvas, the Apsaras, the Vaanars, the Nagas, the Yakshas, and the Rakshasas.

Most people thought the Rakshasas were demons because, four millennia ago, the Rakshasa Warlord waged war against the Seventh Avatar of Lord Vishnu— Lord Ram. However, the Rakshasas were fierce mercenaries and protectors, if allied and raiders- if against- the Devas' vaults.

Dyaus was the King of the Devas at the time of his disappearance.

"My Lady..." the soldier hesitated.

"What is it?" she asked.

"We found a letter in the saddlebag of Lord D—"

Prithvi didn't wait for the young soldier to complete his sentence. She checked the first pocket of the saddlebag and withdrew a greasy roll of parchment in a wooden cylinder. The cylinder had her name in the Tibetan script.

Strange, she wondered.

While she and Dyaus knew Tibetan, he was unlikely to use the language, which could only mean one thing.

He wanted it to remain secret! But why? She wondered.

She opened the scroll, broke the seal and started to read. As she reached the middle, she burst out crying, and her hands started shaking. She finished it and sat with sadness taking over. It contained the message about Dyaus' quest, how the Bhutaganas were pursuing him and that his disappearance could only mean death, for he had been gone six months. This also meant that he would never see his youngest son.

The funeral processions had to take place without the body of Dyaus. The cold Bactrian air was biting Prithvi's cheeks and forehead. Her tears, warm in the beginning, froze on her cheeks. A class of specially trained priests sang hymns to Lord Yama, the God of Death and Dharma, the psychopomp, the first mortal to die, and the King of the Dead.

"My Lady," the head priest said, pointing the urn of the substitute body's ashes towards Prithvi.

She looked at the urn and the stream flowing from the South to the Chakshu River—also known as the Amu Darya in these parts.

"No," she replied.

"But, My Lady!"

"No. Not here. In the Saraswati. In his homeland. In Dyau…"

She couldn't bring herself to say his name.

6 YEARS LATER

3

"Indra?" questioned Prithvi. It had been six years since the demise of Dyaus. Prithvi and the late Dyaus' child, Indra, was a hyperactive kid. He and his two older brothers, Mitra and Varuna, were sent to the famous Gurukul of Guru Brihaspati. It was on a very clear spring morning when Indra, Mitra, and Varuna decided to flood Guru Brihaspati's mud-brick and felt-ceiling hut. Mitra and Varuna, a decade older than Indra, always managed to make Indra take the blame for what happened by bribing him with toys. Today, it was apples.

"*Th*o you want me to *aglee* to…"

"Yes," said Mitra to the lisping and stuttering Indra.

Mitra and Varuna were both sixteen years of age. Almost adults now, their voices had nearly matured. There was fine hair on their upper lips. Varuna had clear, flawless white skin, while Mitra had a slightly reddish tint to his skin.

They set to work, finding small cracks and closing them with clay and plaster. Once done, the boys closed the door and emptied pails of water on the ground. Once they ensured it didn't leak, they jumped out of the window and waited for Brihaspati to open the door. Soon enough, they heard a loud shout.

"Mitra! Varuna!" They walked up innocently to their

Guru with folded hands, "*Namaste,* Guruji. To what do we owe the pleasure?"

Brihaspati angrily pointed out his wet dhoti, the puddle on the floor and his wet sandals.

The boys gasped. "We didn't do anything, Guruji!"

The boys were scared at the prospect of getting punished by their Guru. Nearly five feet eight inches in height, with muscular arms, calloused palms, a huge belly and a greying beard, the rishi was a man of immense knowledge. This was the reason Prithvi appointed him for her son's education. Only the best would do for the future king of the Devas.

However, at this moment, his face seemed redder than his saffron-dyed bark shawl.

"Who did it?" he enquired.

"It *wad* me, *Guluji,*" came a voice in a hushed way.

Mitra and Varuna winked at Indra.

Brihaspati groaned. Whenever he thought he got the boys, Indra took the blame. And he had no proof as to who did it.

"Lady Prithvi!" shouted Brihaspati.

He hoped the boy's fear of his strict mother might make him speak the truth. But he looked unblinkingly into his Guru's eye.

Prithvi walked out of her hut.

After the exile, most Devas lost the palaces and bungalows they owned and lived in huts. The poor people lived in yurts, which meant that in the case of any attack, the exodus of the entire nation was an easy option. Which also meant that all lived equally in similar-sized houses. And so, many Gandharvas, Vaanars and Nagas escaped the North beyond the Uparishyena instead of Persia, the Mediterranean and Egypt to avoid Asura persecution.

The only difference in the queen's hut was that it was slightly bigger and had three rooms.

"What's the problem, Guruji?"

"Your son flooded my hut!"

She knew Indra couldn't do it. But the boys... Well, she didn't know why Indra was taking the blame. Maybe he was bribed. Whatever the case, she decided to take away his toy sword, hoping it would stop.

But it didn't. The following week, a jar of preserved apples disappeared, the blame was taken by Indra, a broken clay jar was found outside Mitra's hut, and Indra had a shining new wooden sword.

However cross he might have appeared at the repeated actions of the boys, Brihaspati had a good laugh about all of it in his hut. He enjoyed the boys' antics when in private. But he knew that they had to be disciplined if they were to become able rulers. So, he kept punishing them, acted cross in front of them and had a good laugh about it in private.

4

"Lord Vritra."

The Assyrian sun burned hard on the army with thirty-thousand strong men who marched East towards the Lands cradled by the Sindhu. Their leader was an unnaturally tall, bronze-skinned man of nearly six feet eleven inches. Though he wore a long white robe, his muscular chest and arms could be seen. His full beard and kohl-lined eyes, their light hazel colour, the pointed earlobes and long canines gave him the appearance of a dragon or a serpent.

"Lord Vritra," the attendant tentatively offered the waterskin to his overlord.

The man took it, gulped some sips, and signalled for his army to stop. The three vertical lines on his forehead from sandal paste and turmeric identified him as a devotee of Lord Narayana, the cosmic, all-encompassing form of Lord Vishnu.

The soldiers stopped at the signal from their master.

"If you retards keep walking at this pace, we might as well let the Devas take Aryavarta," he shouted.

"You all better walk faster tomorrow, or I swear on Lord Vishnu, you shall not get another night's rest. Is that clear?"

"Yes, Lord Vritra."

"Good," the Dragon smiled.

20 YEARS LATER

5

The now twenty-six-year-old Indra had been granted the title of 'Devendra', the Lord of The Devas. Many called him Lord Indra.

Indra's, or, as he was now known, Lord Indra's administration made the Devas the most prosperous they had been since coming out of Aryavarta.

He had introduced the long-lost system of international trade. His traders were given loans by the Royal Treasury and sent to the markets in Kashgar, where they bought silk for cheap and sold it to The Mediterranean at extravagant prices and reaped enormous profits. It was on one such diplomatic visit that Mitra planned to go.

"So, wait, you want to go on a trade mission?"

"That's what I said, Lord Indra," mocked Mitra.

"But you're nobility! You already have all the gold you could ask for!"

"Indra, can I be honest here? I am not going to trade. I am going to meet the Persians."

"What? *Bhratashree*, why?" Indra asked his elder brother.

Mitra sighed, "Do you know of the Bhutaganas?"

Indra was puzzled. The Tribe of Lord Shiva was all about the lore.

"Yes."

"When I was little, around seven or eight, father disappeared. His body was never found. Anyways, yesterday, I entered Mother's hut while she slept. And I read a letter put on her side table. It was written in Tibetan, and you know how I have a knack for that language. Anyways, I read it and it said that…"

Mitra lowered his voice to a whisper.

"It contained a message. It said that our father had gone on 'The Ultimate Quest' and that he would restore the glory of the Devas. He, mother, me, Varuna, and You would be worshipped like Gods in the Sapta-Sindhu. He also mentioned that 'The Vine' is lost. He also…"

Mitra paused as he heard footsteps. As soon as the noise died, Mitra lowered his voice and continued, "He also mentioned that he stole the weapon."

Indra sucked in a deep breath. He was confused. He sat silently and contemplated. "What do you have to do in Persia?"

"Father mentions a weapon hidden away in Persia. Its effects sound pretty magical to me. I mean, a weapon that can decimate an army and yet could be used as a target weapon. He said it was for you to discover. So I'll just get it. For you."

Indra trusted Mitra and Varuna completely. However, he had a nagging question at the back of his mind. What is this magical weapon? What does it look like?

"Have you heard of the *Divyastras?*"

The Divyastras were weapons of mass destruction. Nearly one thousand years ago, a war that involved four million people was fought on the battlefield of Kurukshetra. Originally known as the Kurukshetra War or the Kaurava-

Pandava War, it led to most people's deaths. Hardly a few thousand soldiers barely escaped with their lives. This was due to the power and effect of the Divyastras. Each weapon contained the management of the element or God it was charged with.

"You mean an actual astra?" asked an incredulous Indra.

"Not just any astra. It's known as a Vajra," said Mitra, barely able to contain his smile.

A Vajra was the symbol of the first Devendra, Lord Indra.

"Why do you look so "Thunderstruck", Lord Indra?" joked Mitra, pun intended.

It was widely known that a vajra was an electric weapon. It could produce large-scale electrical fires, like those produced by thunderbolts. It could be hurled through the sky and fall like a meteorite. It could be used to one's advantage to turn a dry area into a blazing inferno.

"No one should know of this."

"It'll be more discreet than what's inside your loincloth," Mitra said.

"All right. I shall make you the Minister of Trade."

"I'll say I'm going to gain first-hand experience."

"May the Trinity grant you success, my brother."

6

The Assyrian army was encamped on the banks of the holy Sindhu, the Western Frontier of the Sapta-Sindhu, the land of seven rivers, also known as Aryavarta, after the legendary heroes of the past, The Aryas.

Vritra stood, overlooking the land of his birth. A sight for sore eyes. He still remembered *the day.*

He accompanied his father to the local market.

He had some dirt on his nose. His mother smiled and wiped it with her shawl. His father went to judge the quality of the muslins. Suddenly, there was a loud commotion on the western side of the market. A merchant's throat was slit. Mlecchas, barbarians from the far west, drew out their swords and massacred the vendors and the customers. The men were all killed, and the women were taken aboard the ships. His father was among the dead. His mother was dragged aboard. Vritra ran. He ran all through the night.

The local Governor's palace was a day's journey away. Nearly two days after the incident, Vritra was sobbing uncontrollably. The palace was almost six hours away. An elderly man saw the sobbing Vritra.

"What happened, boy?" the man asked kindly.

Vritra sobbed.

"Are you hungry?"

The boy nodded.

The man reached into his bag and drew out a laddoo, a ball of sugar and flour, usually eaten as a dessert.

The boy took the offered sweet and ate it ravenously.

"Where are your parents?" the man inquired.

Vritra sobbed and told the man of the incident at the markets.

The man hugged Vritra. He took out three laddoos and wrapped them in the paper. "Who has no one has Lord Vishnu, my child. Remember that. Lord Narayana has a plan for all. Om Namo Narayanaya," chanting, the man departed, giving the boy the laddoos and his shawl. The boy stared after the departed man and whispered within his mind the chant of those loyal to the Great Pervader, the upholder of Dharma (righteousness).

The Governor's palace sent the boy away because of the black onyx pendant on the gold chain around his neck. It marked him as a Kalakeya Asura. Six months later, he was kidnapped by the Mlecchas.

Since that day, the boy has risen rapidly in Sargon the Great's army's ranks after saving the King from a lion. He found his mother in the harem of one of the King's bodyguards. That man was never seen again. On that day began the vengeance of Vritra— the firstborn of the Dragons.

Many of the King's merchants vanished, and nobody took notice. Vritra had now become the apple of Sargon's eye. And the painful subject of his retirement was troubling Sargon more than the one retiring.

"Vritra…" Sargon said with moist eyes.

"Your Highness, I can't fight anymore. Innocent blood is on my hands. I want renunciation. And what better place for a spiritual experience than the land of Melukkha," Vritra referred to the Sapta-Sindhu as it was known in Assyria.

"And you're going to take your soldiers?" asked a puzzled Sargon.

"It's better to be safe than sorry, Your Highness. Political conditions are not so good in Magan and Gandara."

Sargon, who loved Vritra like a son, did not want him to go. Finally giving in, he said, "May Inanna protect you, Vritra", and embraced him tightly.

"May Lord Vishnu protect you, Great King."

Vritra smiled at the turn of events. He could finally exact his revenge on the Governor, who denied him justice all those years ago. He was coming.

7

It had been two weeks since Mitra's departure to Persia. An excuse had been provided by Prithvi's approaching birthday and the need for a delicate gold necklace for her neck.

Indra was arguing over the gold necklace with his mother. Widows were not allowed to wear any jewellery or silk raiment.

"Mother, you know that's a stupid custom to demean women and make them feel guilty," protested Indra.

"No, son, it's the rule. For whatever reason it was made, there's a logic."

"Ugh! Rules, rules, RULES! I am getting it for you! And you can either wear it or give it to a handmaiden for all I care!" shouted Indra, shaking with fury.

"But why?"

"Because I love you!"

Prithvi sighed audibly.

"All right. I'll wear one. But don't get anything too elegant."

"Thank you!"

Prithvi smiled at her son.

"I'm going to feed the dogs."

Indra's two-year-old bitch Sarama had just given birth to two healthy pups. They were named Sharvar and Shyam.

They were named after the legendary hounds of Lord Yama, the brother of Lord Manu, the progenitor of civilisation.

The puppies seemed to love Indra's cows and followed the herds everywhere. It could be said that the pups spent more time with the cows than their mother.

8

The kingdom of Saurashtra was an important hub for the worship of Lord Shiva. The temple of Lord Somnath, a form of Lord Shiva, was visited by thousands of devotees each year.

The area was under the control of the Nagas. The Nagas were primarily agriculturists... They believed in the existence of natural spirits and worshipped snakes. They were great devotees of Lord Shiva. The second Nagaraja, Lord Vasuki-I, was the right-hand man of the third Rudra, Lord Neelkanth.

Right now, however, even Lord Shiva could not help the Nagaraja. Takshak-III was in a dilemma. Helping Vritra cross Saurashtra would mean treason. And the King, if he won, would oust the Nagas out of one of the last safe places they had. On the contrary, denying Vritra the chance to go would result in a battle. And Takshak was outnumbered by a significant margin.

"Great Dragon, it would be inappropriate-"

"You don't have to fight for me, Great Naga. Even if that oversized peacock wins, you won't be harmed."

"But-"

"I have a solution. My army will pretend to lay siege to your fort. You retreat inside. I will place a skeletal force of a few thousand of my soldiers. Even if that fat mongrel wins, you can tell him you were besieged."

Vritra was told never to underestimate his enemy at any cost.

The humid monsoon air was making Takshak sweaty. The dimly-lit conference hall needed a thorough cleaning. But servants cost money—something which the Nagas lacked.

Historically, they were the wealthiest tribe in the Sapta-Sindhu. But, the Kurukshetra War was destructive to the Naga economy. The Nagas were related to Lord Bhimasena and, by extension, the Pandavas, heroes of the Kurukshetra War. They donated vast sums of money to the Pandavas, all of which Lord Karkotak IV, the then Nagaraja did not want returned.

Takshak contemplated the solution. Finally, he sighed. "I shall have to discuss it with my ministers, Lord Vritra."

"Please do, Great Naga."

Takshak signalled a nearby servant with his hand.

"Call the Prime Minister and the General."

Vritra licked his lips and waited for a reply.

His unnatural calmness added to the tense environment in the room. His eerily friendly smile made Takshak sweat harder. He got up and lit two oil lamps while thinking about the man in front of him. There were rumours he was born from a fire.

Two men entered. One was dressed in the white turban, indigo dhoti and sky-blue *angavastra.* He had a handlebar moustache and muscular, battle-scarred arms. The gold armband with a sapphire at the centre indicated him as the commander of the Naga army. Three paste lines on his forehead proudly announced his devotion to Lord Shiva. His jewellery was minimal: serpent ear-studs, the compulsory military armband and a gold chain with a trident pendant, again showing his dedication to the God of Gods, Lord Shiva.

The other man was the complete opposite of the first. He was dressing to show, to flaunt his wealth. He wore a pink turban, violet angavastra and an indigo dhoti. Gold covered what clothes couldn't. His enormous belly, compliments to an unhealthy diet, pasty face, clean-shaven beard, bloodshot eyes, pendulous male breasts, receding hairline and catechu-stained teeth all made him look like the most miserable and stingy trader on the planet.

"My Lord", greeted the men and saluted in the Naga fashion, genuflecting with the right knee on the ground and placing the head on the floor where the King's feet were a moment before.

"Are women allowed in the meeting, Your Highness?" asked Vritra, snorting disgustedly at the Prime Minister.

"Great Dragon, allow me to introduce my most important aides. This is my General Lord Dharma and my Prime Minister Lord V—"

"Lady" corrected Vritra in mock studiousness.

The Prime Minister was trying hard to control his anger. He had never been insulted so. He was being called a woman, that too twice, a weaker being; as per him.

Takshak could sense the bubbling anger within the Prime Minister. Quickly changing the topic, he gave a summary of the meeting.

"Sounds right, My Lord. However, Lord Vritra…" began Dharma in a deep, baritone voice. He hesitated a bit before continuing.

"Will our men be harmed?" asked Dharma.

"My friend, stay out of our way, and my men will try to keep the casualties minimal."

Not convinced, Dharma eyed Vritra suspiciously.

Vritra continued.

"All right. Here's the offer. A hundred gold coins per body."

That did it. Takshak quickly pulled out a piece of paper and quickly scribbled something. He dipped his signet ring in the inkpot and marked his seal, the cobra, with a spread hood.

Vritra scanned the text on the paper. Satisfied, he dipped his signet ring in his signature crimson ink and stamped it on the paper.

"With Lord Shiva as the witness," said Takshak.

"With Lord Shiva and Lord Vishnu as the witnesses," whispered Vritra.

Glory to Lord Narayana, whispered the firstborn of The Dragons to himself.

9

Mitra sat alone in his hut. It had been eight weeks since he left for Persia. He himself, Brihaspati and twenty soldiers set up camp in a discreet village. Yesterday, he received a letter from Varuna saying that he had been appointed the Chief Judicial Officer of the Devas. The very post held by Lord Yama many millennia ago. Mitra couldn't have been happier.

For him, however, the last few weeks had been disastrous. He could neither find the gold necklace nor the weapon.

He sat on the comfortable chair and adjusted his underwear in the not-so-comfortable Persian robe. He sat back again, but the underwear still troubled him.

"The hell with this!" he cursed and wrenched off the gown. He was clad in just a white loincloth. His extremely fit body was adorned with bruises. While Varuna preferred using swords, that too in a pair, Mitra practised wrestling and boxing.

He sat back again and picked up a manuscript. Mitra preferred to spend his free time reading and learning new languages. The manuscript was in Old Persian, and he could decipher the title from the cover—Preparation of Haoma.

Puzzled, Mitra started to read. The first chapter seemed to be made up of hymns to the mighty Haoma plant, which is golden, which gives the haoma juice, which increases strength, speed, endurance, enhances beauty, has no adverse effects and is an aphrodisiac.

The second chapter dealt with the preparation of haoma. As Mitra was reading this, his mind wandered. He read about the haoma vine.

Vines. The truth hit him like a tonne of bricks. *The vine from Father's letter!*

"Guards!" shouted Mitra.

A few moments later, two guards appeared.

"Yes, Lord Mitra."

"Tell Brihaspati ji to come to my tent. No, he hasn't committed a crime!" he said as the guards unsheathed their swords.

Meanwhile, he changed his attire to a formal orange dhoti and blue shawl.

Brihaspati came in a few moments later.

"Why have you summoned me so late, Lord Mitra?" enquired Brihaspati.

"Guru Brihaspati" Mitra bowed down to touch Guru Brihaspati's feet in the traditional Sapta-Sindhu way.

"May you be victorious in all your endeavours," blessed Brihaspati.

"Have a seat, Guruji," requested Mitra.

Brihaspati sat down on the proffered seat.

"Guruji, something on my mind has been troubling me."

Brihaspati waited patiently.

"Guruji, is there some plant, or vine, a herb that has… I don't know, some magical effects? Maybe increase your lifespan? Make you immortal?"

Though the question was asked casually, Brihaspati's expression changed from patience to worry to fear.

"Lower your voice" croaked a fearful Brihaspati.

"By the laws of my tribe, I can never lie or deny someone an answer, for my vow of spreading true knowledge is sacred. We are to spread knowledge. Don't ask me about my tribe now. I shall reveal it to you later."

Mitra watched as his Guru, someone he had learned to admire for his bravery, shook like a hyena seeing a lion.

"There is one. It's known as the Soma."

Mitra nearly dropped the manuscript from his hands. Sanskrit words usually made their way into Old Persian, where they were changed to roll them easily on the Persian tongues. So, the sound for 's' became 'h'. So, the Sindhu River became Hindu, Sarasvati became Haraxvati, and logically, Soma would become Homa.

Brihaspati continued, "It's made from the Somalata plant. It's a vine and grows high in the mountains. It's rare, very, very rare."

"Tell me more about it," said an intrigued Mitra.

10

Vritra's cavalry surrounded the Nagas' concentric fort. They were at enough distance for the mounted archers and spear-throwers to attack but far enough to avoid the crossfire and boiling oil, and anyway, most archers were inside the inner rink, which made arrows unstable.

However, since some soldiers had to be left at the fort to make the trick look like an actual siege, the mounted archers had to be left behind; they were the only unit which gave the Assyrians the upper hand.

"My Lord..." The Assyrian General Shushna saluted.

"What is it, General?"

"My Lord, the mounted archer corps are the unit which gives us the upper hand in the battle. We can't leave them here to waste away while our soldiers face defeat."

Vritra liked this impulsive restlessness of Shushna, always focusing on the crucial task at hand.

"Tell me, General. Do we have to place our corps here or give the enemy the illusion that our main army is posted here?"

The General understood and smiled.

"What are your orders, my Lord?" asked the grinning Shushna.

"Get me two thousand inexperienced riders. They are going to pretend to be the main cavalry. The element of surprise is with us. We can use the mounted archers as the surprise element. Surely, the King's spies must have informed him about the mounted cavalry. And anyway, we did pretend to put up a fight—Five hundred Nagas dead."

"Six hundred, my Lord."

"Get ready. We leave for the capital tomorrow."

"Yes, My Lord. Narayana is with us."

"He's everywhere, General."

And with this, the General exited the crimson war tent of his master.

11

Brihaspati gazed outside the tent. The guards were asleep. The thorn hedge was intact. Brick walls protected the village. The village was unlikely to be attacked by anyone except travelling bandits.

"All right. The Soma-making process begins with the Soma vine. It is called the Somalata. It is found in the high mountains. Its potential is such that it can make a man live for centuries. Have you heard of the Eight Immortals?"

The Asht-Chiranjeevi were a group of eight immortals who had lived through the ages. Lord Hanuman, Lord Ram's most fervent devotee, was one of them.

"The Somalata is painstakingly collected from the Himalayas. Its juices are extracted, pressed and mixed. Either water, honey, milk or yoghurt will do. However, it is poisonous and bitter and can make one sick for quite some time. So, Dhatura- another poison which neutralises it- is mixed with milk, and is used. Hydromel is also to be used. The Bhutaganas are tasked with protecting the secret of the Soma. It is the sacred duty of the Rudra."

Mitra couldn't breathe.

"Guruji, do the Persians-"

"Well, yes. They do, but the Somalata is difficult to find. It's rarely done. Wha... how do you know?"

Mitra showed the manuscript to Brihaspati.

"I see."

"Did... did Father go to search for the Somalata before he vanished, I mean?"

Brihaspati stared in admiration at his former student. *The boy is smart.*

"I can't lie to you. So I'll tell the truth. Your father went to the Himalayas to search for it. It had rarely been seen. Only the Rudra and the Bhutaganas possess it. So, he went to search for it. I expected him to return empty-handed. However, he never returned. So I enquired in the town he was last seen in. Coincidentally, the Rudra's private vault was there. The Bhutaganas told me that he had attempted to rob the vault and got away with a dry bush."

A guard entered, "Lord Mitra!"

12

"My Lord, a bull has been disturbing the local villagers. He killed two soldiers right now."

"You idiots can't even kill a bull?" snorted Mitra.

"But, my Lord—"

"What?"

Mitra was confused, but then he remembered. Cattle were considered sacred in Aryavarta. Cows were worshipped like Goddesses. Cows were *aghnya i.e.,* they couldn't be killed.

"Oh, for the Gods' sake."

Mitra removed his shawl. He tightened his dhoti, wore his sandals, and walked out into the darkness.

Not seeing the bull anywhere, he enquired.

"Where's the damn beast?"

Two soldiers pointed out a hole in the wall. The thorn bushes had been torn apart, probably in agony from the thorns.

"Get my horse."

A guard went to untether Mitra's horse. Sitting comfortably on the brocade saddle, he thought of a sword.

"Get my sword."

Most soldiers in the Sapta-Sindhu preferred having a curved blade with one edge on it. It was lighter, easily wielded with one hand, and was comfortable on horseback. Mitra, however, preferred a double-edged, pointed and straight sword. Curved swords are suitable for thrusting, but straight, pointed blades go well for stabbing. Mitra unsheathed his sword, threw down the scabbard, and went after the hoof prints and dung trail.

Mitra continued for a mile or so in the southwest direction. He reached a hill and stopped his horse. On the base of the hill, a small town was present. Looking closely, he realised they didn't have the typical Persian features of white skin and hooked noses. They looked… they looked like monkeys. That was the word Mitra had thought of. They had upturned noses, dark skin, fur-like thick hair and a few even seemed to have tails. Their disfigured jaws and hairless upper lips made them look… like mixtures of lions and langurs.

Vaanars, thought Mitra.

The Vaanars were a tribe that lived in Southern Aryavarta. They lived around Mount Rishyamuka, Lake Pampa and the Tungabhadra River.

They had high rates of a type of mutation, resulting in disfigured jaws, tails and extra fingers and toes. However, Vaanar physicians were well-equipped to make the disease non-lethal.

The Vaanars worshipped Lord Hanuman and the forces of nature. Their banner had a monkey on it.

That would explain the bull, thought Mitra.

Since cows were sacred in the Sapta-Sindhu, the Vaanars allowed the bull to terrorise them.

Mitra rode into the village.

The scene that greeted him was not one of joy . Dead bodies were being cremated. Hymns to Lord Yama, Lord Shiva and the dead were being chanted.

Seeing the mounted warrior, a few men moved aside. A mother who was cremating her young son watched with tearful eyes as Mitra dismounted, bowed low and began to pray for the dead Vaanar's soul.

"How long will you face the torture of this beast?" asked Mitra in Sanskrit. He hoped that the Vaanars might know the ancient language. He got a response from an old man.

"We are from the Sapta-Sindhu. We can't just kill a bull."

"Lord Krishna killed the bull, Vatsa." Said Mitra.

"But we're not Lord Krishna."

"It's a Warrior's duty to protect the meek. I can't just let you die. Not on my watch," said Mitra.

Saying so, he picked up his sword and asked, "Where is the beast?"

The old man stared in awe at the amazingly fit body of the warrior. He pointed to a field.

The gigantic, hulking beast slowly ate the wheat. Almost as if it was taunting the one who grew the crops. The beast was nearly six-and-a-half feet tall. He had massive feet-long horns on the side of his head. The horns didn't curve but went straight and bent in the middle, then recurved to show long tips just above the beast's eyes. A band of five archers would have struggled to take on the beast. Mere arrows wouldn't injure its hide. The hump on its back was reminiscent of the zebu. However, the dewlap, very typical of the zebus, was missing. It grunted.

Mitra was awe-struck at the magnificence of the beast. He knew that the bull was not an ordinary zebu.

Aurochs, thought Mitra.

Mitra contemplated sneaking up from behind. *No,* he thought. There was no bravery in that. Also, he had to set an example.

Finally facing real competition, he decided to wrestle the bull. A fight to the death. The *vrisha* against the *naravrishabha*.

A bull against the bull among the men.

Mitra roared. The bull snorted and ignored it. Mitra roared again. This time, it was louder. The bull turned and looked at the intruder. Mitra burst into a run and threw his sword on the ground. The clang of the metal startled the bull as he ran towards the new threat. Mitra sidestepped and avoided the point of the horns.

The bull, maddened with testosterone and angry at being duped, increased its pace and tried to gut Mitra. Mitra sidestepped and grabbed hold of the hump that was the bull's blind spot. Desperately struggling to escape the unseen threat, the bull started shaking violently.

This would have made an ordinary man fall face first and get trampled by the beast. But Mitra was no normal man. He was The Bull amongst Men. He held on.

The Vaanars watched in awe. They had read about the game played in the Vaanar homeland. It was known as Jallikattu. In it, a bull with gold coins tied at its horns was released, and a man struggled to hold on to its hump.

Mitra made the bull exert itself. His strategy was to exhaust it so Mitra could kill it quickly.

Sure enough, the bull sat down some minutes later and tried to regain its breath. Mitra dismounted and made the bull chase him. However, the exhausted beast was strolling towards Mitra. Mitra quickly changed position, sidestepped, pirouetted and picked up his sword.

The bull, exhausted, sat down with an audible thump. He sensed that the man got what he came for. It was partially true. The man had got what he came for.

He went close to the bull.

"Forgive me," apologised a teary-eyed Mitra.

The regret and guilt of killing such a magnificent animal took over the bravery and manliness of having to kill such a mighty beast.

However, he steeled himself. He wiped the tears from his eyes. He had to set an example. Tears had to be hidden. He gripped the blade tightly.

The bull was sitting in the mud very quietly. It didn't protest at the closeness of the human. It behaved almost like a little calf. It seemed to sense that its end was near, making it all the more difficult for Mitra to do the deed. He grabbed onto the hump, startling the beast. It stood up and shook. Mitra stabbed the beast in the gut. Mitra would be crushed under two thousand pounds of pure rage if it rolled over. The agonised beast fell to the ground on the side where the sword was embedded. Its falling led to the sword going deeper and piercing the beast's lungs, ribs, heart and ultimately, spine.

The fall allowed Mitra to go away. He waited for the beast to die. Finally, it sputtered blood in a final cough and went to the elements.

Mitra roared to announce his success. The villagers were finally free from the menace.

"What is your name, Great Warrior?" enquired the Vaanar headman.

"I am Mitra."

"Meet your saviour, Ahura Mithra!"

Ahura was the Avestan title for deified heroes or concepts. Ahura Mazda, or Lord Wisdom, was the supreme God of the Persians.

Before even Lord Manu's time, Asura was originally a title for the nobility. Later, it was corrupted to mean demon in the age of The Devas. Asura and Ahura were the same.

The Asuras were originally well-meaning people, exiled from Persia to the Sapta-Sindhu. Differing customs and tongues made the Devas hostile to them. Their pointless wars carried on for centuries until the Devas' exile.

A legend was born. The legend of Ahura Mithra, the Slayer of The Bull.

13

The King of Saurashtra was sitting with the letter he had just finished reading. The news he had received from his incredibly incompetent information network was disturbing. Some Assyrian warlord had crossed the Sindhu and moved south to Naga territory. The bastard had even laid siege to the Naga fort at Lothal.

Lothal housed the most important docks of the Sapta-Sindhu since Lord Krishna's famed Dwarika. A siege to Saurashtra's ports would mean that a potential escape and trade route had been blocked.

Wrinkles were stretched across his forehead as he enquired about the spy.

"And the river?"

"Blocked, My Lord. Warships in the river stop the Nagas from escaping."

"Damn!" cursed the King.

"What's the bloody cur's name?" asked the agitated King.

"Someone called Vritra, my Lord. He seems to be an Asura."

Just then, a messenger walked in.

"Your Highness!"

"WHAT THE BLOODY HELL! CAN'T YOU SEE WE'RE DISCUSSING THE WAR HERE?" thundered the enraged King.

Shocked at his master's anger, the servant muttered a hasty apology, left the letter on the table, and left wordlessly.

The King checked the letter. It was addressed to him. He quickly scanned it. The letter seemed to be written with some viscous red substance. He sniffed it. *Blood. By the gods! He is a madman!*

The King clutched his *Shivalinga* pendant tightly.

Most foreigners interpreted the lingam as merely a phallic stump. But, to the enlightened one, it was much more than that. It was a symbol of creation.

The stump, the lingam, symbolised Lord Shiva, the masculine energy, the mind. And the pedestal was the yoni, the symbol of the feminine energy, the body. Their union was creation.

The King saw the seal at the end of the document. On it was written 'The Firstborn of the Dragons'.

He burnt the letter.

Load of horse shit, he thought.

He was preparing for war and peace was not an option.

14

Indra sat alone in his hut as he read the letter from Mitra. He was glad to read of his elder brother's killing of the bull. As he turned the sheet, he read of Mitra's new discovery. The more he read, the more it disturbed him.

So, Father was after the Soma!

His eyes teared up as he read about the Bhutaganas. As he made a silent promise to himself to complete his father's unfinished task, he thought better of it and asked his mother.

He grabbed a white muslin angavastra and rushed off towards his mother's quarters.

Prithvi was looking at a portrait of Dyaus, watery-eyed.

"Mother," Indra asked permission to enter.

"Come in."

Prithvi quickly wiped her tears, put down the portrait and smiled a watery smile at Indra.

Indra went and sat by Prithvi. He looked at the portrait of his Father. He had the carcass of a tiger at his feet. He seemed unnaturally tall. Or maybe the tiger was small. His eyes, almond-shaped, were just like Indra's.

The artist had captured his glowing visage, muscled torso, burly arms and potbelly. His beard and hair were still black, though they had begun to grey near the temples. A gold headband looked majestic on his head. An armband and a gold chain enhanced his appearance and showed his wealth while not making him look too showy. A trefoil-patterned shawl ran from his right hand to his left shoulder. His face showed a calm character and a gritty, determined look about him. It looked as if Indra was staring through a time portal at himself. Tears escaped his eyes and flowed down freely at the bedsheet.

"He was just like you."

"How…how did he…"

"I-I don't want you involved in it, son. I know you. You are going to involve yourself with it. I… I don't want you to die, son."

It is time for plan B. He decided to take her by surprise.

"Why were the Bhutaganas after him, mother?"

"Wha… how did you… Indra, my child, listen. I won't put your life at risk by telling you."

"I have my sources, mother."

Prithvi was in a dilemma. She did not want to risk her son's life by telling him the truth. On the contrary, she did not want him to get incomplete information and form his own opinions of Dyaus.

"All right, listen. I met your father when I was young. I was nearly sixteen then. Your father was seventy."

Seeing his thunderstruck demeanour, she continued, "Have you heard of Soma?"

Indra relaxed a bit. The changes in his expression convinced Prithvi that he knew it. Yet, another reason for her to worry.

"He was one of the best Devendras. Under his rule, the Devas commanded a huge part of Bactria. It even included the Aparanta region."

The Aparanta region was home to the martial clan of the Baloch.

"Your Father was from the Prajapati tribe. The Devas were indebted to the Prajapatis. They were responsible for the Devas' departure after the Kurukshetra war. Moreover, my father was convinced that the marriage would be successful. After all, Dyaus was The Head of Brahma."

Indra stared in awe at his mother. Being a representative of the Holy Trinity was a rare honour

"How did he..."

"He made the technology of the Soma available to all worthy Devas. Before that, it was restricted to a few rishis, nobles and the Devendra."

"But, the Bhutaganas..."

"To make the Soma, the Somalata had to be used in ample quantities. Rapid production and consumption led to its extinction in Bactria. Dhatura and Hydromel are also expensive ingredients. The Deva treasuries were running out of money. So Dyaus went to the Bhutaganas. However, the previous Rudra, Kshetrapaal, had taken *sanyas.* He had even renounced speech. The new Rudra, Bhairav, was not a friend of your father's. He did not allow him to take the Somalata, even though he had more than he needed."

The Bhutaganas owned Somalata plantations near Mount Kailash. It was rumoured they lived for centuries. One of Lord Shiva's titles is Maha Mrityunjay— the great conqueror of death. Living up to his reputation as Lord Shiva's representative, the Rudra's responsibility was to provide his tribe members with a long and healthy life.

Indra and Prithvi's conversation was cut short by a loud sound of stampeding animals. Indra rushed out to see his cows being led away by riders with whips: a loud crack, a painful grumble from a cow and an increase in speed. Indra saw a banner through the dim lights of the riders' torches. The green flag depicted a red dog.

"Panis!"

The Panis were an Asura tribe. They lived a week away from New Amaravati. They were a mercantile tribe. They tricked their Mesopotamian customers and reaped undeserved profits. They were usurers. They did not share their undeserved wealth with anyone.

The cows disappeared in a few moments. Five thousand cows were a lot of wealth for the Devas. And for the Panis.

"GENERAL!" shouted a visibly distressed Indra.

After a few clangs, some muttering and cursing appeared a balding man with a sword in hand. Dressed in a simple sarong, black shawl, leather sandals and breastplate, the General bowed down to Indra with a sword in hand.

"General, the Panis have taken away all the cattle of the royal sheds."

"What are my orders, Lord Devendra?"

"Prepare the Maruts. We ride at dawn."

15

The King of Saurashtra stared out of the balcony. He had come a long way from being the governor of a local town to the King of Saurashtra.

The previous king's oldest nephew had no chance of being the King. However, both of the previous king's sons had been killed in a war, leading to the King taking sanyas and the throne going to his brother.

A soldier entered.

"My Lord, the enemy is assembling. They are twenty miles down south of us."

He sighed.

"Arouse the soldiers immediately. Get them in formation. What news from the Nagas?"

"My King, they are still besieged in their fort. It seems they are killing all the messaging pigeons that fly out. The last scroll came two weeks back."

"All right. I don't think the Nagas may help us. Get me the General."

"Yes, my Lord."

Half an hour later, a brown-skinned man with a well-maintained beard entered. His oiled and curled moustache sat symmetrically on his lips. Long, curly hair fell from his military helmet with the General's logo around his shoulders.

Muscles lined his chest and arms. A gold chain with a tiny idol of Lord Hanuman as a pendant adorned his neck.

The General folded his hands into a namaste and bowed low to the King.

"General, arrange fifty-thousand soldiers in a *chakravyuha* fifteen miles south of the fort."

A chakravyuha was a military formation. In it, troops were arranged in seven concentric circles. It was one of the most challenging formations to breach. And one of the most difficult to form.

"My Lord, what is the enemy's position?"

"Twenty miles south, General."

"Should we try to attack them from the Fort itself?"

"No. A siege would be disastrous. It could last for years. Our men would be demoralised."

The General was in deep contemplation. The enemy seemed formidable. After all, seventy thousand soldiers, plus the five thousand at the Naga fort, from Assyria to Saurashtra, were not something everyone could easily manage.

"A chakravyuha, my Lord?" enquired the General.

"A chakravyuha in the centre. It must be surrounded by two phalanxes of fifteen thousand men on each side. The main aim is to block his way. Even if he does succeed, twenty thousand soldiers stay in the fort with me."

"My Lord, there is a problem."

"What is it?"

"My Lord, only seventy thousand soldiers are available right now. The fort of the Nagas has fifty thousand soldiers, which, by treaty, are bound to assist us in wartime. However, we don't have enough troops because they cannot assist us."

The King clutched his Shiva pendant tightly.

"Is there no other way?" he finally asked.

"My Lord, we can ask for a truce."

"NO! I AM THE DESCENDANT OF LORD RAM! OF LORD MANU AND OF LORD VIVASVAN!I AM NOT GOING TO BEG FOR PEACE FROM AN ASURA! THAT TOO, A MLECCHA! PREPARE THE TROOPS! LEAVE FIVE HUNDRED MEN, GATHER THE REST AND ARRANGE THEM!" thundered the King.

The General ran out to obey the orders.

The King stared at the retreating General.

16

"Lord Mitra, Guru Brihaspati requests an audience."

It had been six months since Mitra's killing of the bull. He had to send a letter to Indra every week. He forgot a few times, so Indra sent Varuna to check.

However, it had been three weeks since Mitra's last message. However, no one came to check. Mitra was contemplating sending a servant to check right when the soldier announced the arrival of Brihaspati.

He bowed low to Brihaspati. Brihaspati had a triumphant look about him.

"Salutations, Prince."

"How may I assist you, Guruji?"

Brihaspati played with his beard.

"Prince, do you know how the Vajra works?"

Mitra thought for a second.

"No, Guruji."

Brihaspati smiled. He then explained the complex mechanics behind the ancient thunderbolt.

"There is a crystal near the Chakshu in the Uparisyena mountains. If it is placed in a magnetic field, it can produce electricity. This electricity can be used to kill and even set fire to entire forests at once!"

"Where is the crystal?"

"We must search for it."

"What does it look like?"

"It looks a bit like a white stone in the crudest form. When polished, however, it looks like a diamond."

"And the magnet?"

"Easy to find. I'll get it."

"All right, Guruji. But nobody must know about this."

Brihaspati nodded and left the tent. Mitra stared in deep contemplation at the letter from Dyaus.

The riders had been riding for nearly two hours. The Bactrian heat was taking its toll on the riders, and soon, one fell face-first on the sand. The lead rider turned back and stopped her horse close to the fallen man.

"Halt!" ordered the woman.

Commander Rodasi was the leader of the Maruts. The Maruts were the personal bodyguard troops of the Devendra. Armed with heavy battle axes and gilded spears, they were often used as a last resort in most battles. The Devas had never lost a battle when the Maruts got involved.

Rodasi removed the veil, protecting her face from the elements. A beautiful woman back in the day , age had got the better of her. Muscly, battle-scarred arms and the bow strapped to her back proudly announced her rank as a warrior.

The standard golden Marut breastplate, a gilded helmet, crimson dhoti and war boots were a rare honour given to a few worthy Devas. And even lesser women had the privilege of receiving the same.

Two Maruts picked up the unconscious rider. They sprinkled water on his face. One went to fetch his horse. When the fallen man gained consciousness, his feet were tied to the stirrups. His buttocks adjusted uncomfortably on the saddle. The Marut tried to straighten the unfortunate piece of cloth stuck in the space between his buttocks. But his hands were tied to the reins with some cord.

"Keep riding!" ordered Rodasi.

Indra stared at the commotion behind him.

This is going to be a long journey.

17

The Sarasvati was the holiest of all rivers in The Land of Seven Rivers. The Saurashtra capital of Dholavira was located on its banks. Canals had been cleverly dug to transport the water into the city.

The army of Saurashtra was arranged early in the morning. A Chakravyuha, or Padmavyuha, had been arranged before sunrise. Soldiers were not allowed to wear warm clothing as the comfort might lull them to sleep. The air was tense.

Suddenly, loud drumbeats were heard in the morning. Three war elephants, finely armoured in steel plates, emerged from the south. Two chariots flanked each elephant.

The King stared at the three war elephants two miles south. Maybe it was just the Assyrians.

As he kept staring, he realised the elephants' howdahs didn't seem like the ones his army was sitting on. They were like little castles.

By the gods! Persian elephantry! he figured.

The Persian elephant corps were the most famous in all of the world.

The howdahs were almost like small turrets, protecting the archers inside. The elephants were also well-trained. They didn't run amok and destroy their own armies. The elephants had scimitars attached to their tusks.

He stared at the Assyrian standing atop a chariot, Vritra. He was dressed in a black dhoti, crimson sash and blue angavastra. A crown that doubled as a helmet sat atop his head. Two gleaming black horns came out of the sides. A black onyx pendant signifying his Kalakeya lineage was hanging from the gold chain around his neck.

The chariot sped towards the King of Saurashtra. The alarmed King ordered the frontline soldiers to raise their spears and bar him from coming.

Vritra smiled. His aura was enough to scare the king. He quickly pulled out a white flag of truce. He threw down the crossbow and raised his hands in surrender. The chariot stopped a few feet in front of the King. The King eased his soldiers and went to meet the attacker. The General rode behind.

"So, you're the King of Saurashtra?"

"I am a descendant of Lord Manu, you usurer. Not like you! Your weakling ancestors begged for mercy at our feet. Hayagreeva, Hiranyaksh, Hiranyakashyap, all those bastards got what they deserved."

"I'm not here to discuss lineage, Your Highness."

"Then what are you here for?"

"Revenge,"

"What revenge? What did I do to you? I never even went to your homeland; you piece of dung!" spat the King.

"Does Assyria look like my homeland, King?"

The King stared. Vritra did not seem like a Mesopotamian. He looked unnaturally...like a Sapta-Sindhu native with his coppery-bronze skin and curled moustache that sat atop a black beard.

"What do you want?"

The flag waved more intensely in the wind. It almost seemed like it was giving a signal to the army. Out of the howdahs flew out a shower of arrows. The General and the King were shot down by arrows in rapid succession. The General died instantly while the King was pinned to the ground with arrows.

"You used to be the governor of a town near Lothal, remember?" asked Vritra.

The King nodded.

Vritra pressed his hobnailed sandal deep into the man's face. He screamed.

"Goodbye, Your Highness!" chuckled Vritra.

He plunged a dagger into the man's chest. The man stiffened, then went limp.

Vritra smiled at the lifeless corpse. Vengeance had been served.

The terrified army threw down their weapons and raised their hands in surrender.

"All Hail Vritra, the Firstborn of the Dragons, the new King of Saurashtra!" shouted Vritra's charioteer.

18

Ten soldiers standing on the mountain were looking around. They were desperately struggling to find some crystals. Their leader, Mitra, was himself searching for them. In the rocks of the Uparishyena, the glass-like crystals would be easily discerned.

However, their rarity was why they had been searching for six days…

"Spread out and search. Two go to the foot of the mountains. Four of you scour the valley. Rest stay here," ordered Mitra.

"Yes, Lord Mitra."

Judging by the sky's hue, the Sun God would call it a day in less than an hour.

"Wait! You two," he pointed to two soldiers on the mountaintop.

"Erect tents and prepare a fence. Also, light a fire."

"Yes, Lord Mitra."

The soldiers rushed off to obey.

Mitra wiped the sweat off his brow, picked up the pickaxe, and resumed digging.

19

The riding party was in sight of the Pani Citadel.

The Panis were the Northernmost Asura tribe. They were the foremost persecutors of the Devas and their allies after the Kurukshetra War. Having commanded six cities in the past, their rule was now solely over the Mehrgarh fort.

They tried siege tactics on the Deva fort in Amaravati, only to be repelled by the Maruts. While they were busy in the north, their other Citadels were captured by other jealous Asura sub-tribes. The Panis were essentially traders. So, it didn't come as a surprise when the other Asura sub-tribes captured Pani towns.

It was too late by the time they realised it, but still managed to hold on to Mehrgarh.

Mehrgarh was spread over three-quarters of a mile. The fort consisted of a Citadel, the lower town and a cemetery. Asura funerary ceremonies were different from those of other tribes.

The body was buried rather than cremated. It was also supposed to be kept intact.

Another wall surrounded the Citadel itself. This not only reinforced the city but also added to the beauty.

Mostly, the Asuras in the Sapta-Sindhu did not have a system of Kingship. Dictators took charge frequently. When without one, democracy was the form of government. The Citadel was home to the Council of Elders.

Indra and the Maruts stared at the Fortress.

"We must first locate the cows, Lord Devendra," said Rodasi.

Indra nodded. He pulled the reins and turned his horse back. He handed the reins to a Marut, dismounted and went to the empty chariot that Indra's charioteer, , was driving. He was tired and thus went to the chariot and sat down cross-legged.

"We shall release Sarama at night, Rodasi. She will track the cows. She will lead us to them." Indra said, referring to his bitch, Sarama.

20

It had been two months since Vritra became the King of Saurashtra. Since then, the Saurashtrians, the Nagas, the Eastern Chandravanshis and many other tribes had willingly submitted themselves to him.

His empire now stretched from the northern banks of the Narmada in the south up till Avantika, westwards to the Kingdom of Matsya and continuing north to the city of Harappa.

The now two-million-strong army of Vritra made a formidable adversary. To declare his supremacy over the other nearby kingdoms, Vritra performed a Rajasuya Ashwamedha Yagna.

A yagna referred to a ritual fire sacrifice. Energies of ancient Gods deified heroes were invoked with sacred chants or Mantras. In the Rajasuya Ashwamedha, a horse was made to walk through neighbouring kingdoms. If the horse passed unhindered, it signified that the conductor of the yagna was now the overlord of that place. If not, total decimation.

Vritra's horse passed through the lands to the East. From Mahishmati and Chedi. Those kingdoms were now under his dominion.

After conquering the lands, the horse was ritually sacrificed along with a gelded ram. The meat was given to the flame, Lord Agni, the god of fire.

It had been a week since the yagna ceremony. Vritra was standing on the balcony of his new palace. He had shifted the capital to Kalibangan, the Black Fort. It was believed to be the birthplace of the First Lord Brahma— Lord Hiranyagarbha. The older town was the original birthplace of Lord Hiranyagarbha. The newer town was the main centre of social life. The older one, however, still held some significance, albeit a reduced and spiritual one.

Shushna entered.

"You called, My Lord?"

"Yes, General. I was thinking of something."

It was late at night. Shushna had just woken up.

The new palace had been built facing the Saraswati, the holiest river in the Sapta-Sindhu.

"General, the subjects aren't happy with the Asura rule, are they?"

Saurashtra had been the only region in the Sapta-Sindhu not under the dominion of the Asura empire.

"No, my liege."

Vritra took in a deep breath.

"Any revolts?"

"Two, Your Highness. One near Surkotda today itself."

"You remember our ancestors, General? Lord Hiranyaksh and the other great Asura kings?"

"Yes, my Lord," replied a quizzical Shushna, wondering where Vritra was going with this.

"Lord Hiranyaksh caused a massive flood during Lord Varaha's time."

"Yes, I remember. It nearly submerged the whole world."

"That was in another age, General. In this age, the waters must be stopped."

The General was still confused.

"We shall tax the waters. Give the orders. We will dam the rivers. They are the key to control them. Get me the Chief Engineer."

The General abruptly saluted and rushed off to call the Chief Engineer.

A legend was born—the legend of Vritra, the Dragon of Drought.

21

Two weeks had elapsed since Mitra's search for the electric crystals had begun. The effect had not affected the men so much as him. He had not received a letter from home for quite a long time.

He believed that Amaravati was in trouble. However, Brihaspati had advised him against marching off to Amaravati by himself. He did not want any distractions.

"Lord Mitra, we found something at the base of the hill," a soldier said.

Quickly adjusting his shawl, he trotted behind the man. Green-coloured, glass-like stones lay embedded in the black ground. Mitra carefully used his pickaxe to separate the stones from the ground. The rocks were embedded deeper in the ground than Mitra expected. Mitra extracted a fist-sized rock without producing even a small crack in the surface. He rubbed it against his silk dhoti to gain proof of its identity. To his happiness, it created a zapping sound, a small light, making the hair on his arms stand on end.

"Dig out all such stones," ordered Mitra.

Lightning was once again under the control of the Devas.

22

It was two hours after midnight. Most of the inhabitants of that lone city in the Gandhara region had gone to sleep. Smells of wine and merrymaking were coming from a few taverns situated side by side. A well-bred hound was standing in the street, right at the crossroad. Her erect ears, long and slender legs, golden fur and superior sense of smell all pointed to Deva's hunting hound ancestry.

Right now, her nose was focused on the task for which her master had dragged her all the way to Mehrgarh. Finding Indra's stolen cows.

Kidnapping cattle, or *gau-harana,* was the easiest way to provoke a war or simply to assert dominance. In a pastoral civilisation, cattle were the most important animals.

Especially in the Sapta-Sindhu, where cattle were considered sacred. Spiritual, economic, humanitarian and ecological reasons all combined to form the taboo against killing cattle, hence their elevated status.

The bitch picked up the scent. It was coming from the Citadel. She burst into a brisk trot and reached the bronze gate. It was not closed yet.

Two guards were dozing off, their spears embedded in the ground. The warmth of the torches and the warm shawls on their torsos lulled them to sleep. They wore blue woollen *lungis* and leather breastplates.

The Panis worshipped a local deity who rode a dog. Therefore, dogs were sacred.

There were even rituals in which the Panis publicly acknowledged a dog, who recently gave birth, as their sister and to protect the newborn puppies as he would his nephews and nieces.

Sarama sniffed the two men. One reeked of wine and the other of sweat. As she sniffed the other man, she sneezed loud enough to wake the drunk.

"Wh… Who goes there?" he inquired, drawing out his sword. The sober guard also woke up.

"Oh! It's just a dog," said the drunk.

The sweaty guard stared at the drunk. His precious sleep was disturbed. The drunk muttered a hasty apology. The stinkpot shooed Sarama and went back to sleep.

Sarama entered the Citadel, quiet as a mouse. She turned left and continued for a few feet, and a huge cattle shed prevented her from going further.

Sarama ran out faster than she came in. She passed the two guards, continued on the road, ran down the southern highway at the intersection, turned right, and exited the city. She ran for a mile, never stopping and turned around the hillock behind which were hidden the Maruts, Commander Rodasi, and Indra.

She halted four feet away from the Marut horses and began to bark.

"Shhh… Quiet, Sarama!" whispered Rodasi.

"Commander Rodasi, she has found the cows," said Indra, turning to Rodasi.

"Are you sure, Lord Devendra?" asked a doubtful Rodasi.

"I'm positive, Commander. Sarama is a trained Deva hound. She would come back only if she has found the cattle."

Rodasi eyed the two puppies, who ran out of a hole to feed. Sarama was suckling them. She had a tender expression on her face.

A happy mother's face, thought Rodasi.

Her eyes began to tear up as she remembered her miscarriage.

Two Mlecchas with axes had entered her home. They hacked her husband with an axe. As they entered the main bedroom, Rodasi armed herself with her husband's dagger. The Mlecchas laughed at the armed woman.

She tried to stab one of them, but the opponent was neither pregnant nor a young girl. He grabbed her arm and twisted it viciously behind her back. She tried to scream. But he caught her mouth.

They tied her to the bed and removed her robe. She couldn't scream. They banged her head repeatedly against the butt of their swords. She lost consciousness.

She woke up on a soft white bed in an unknown room. A person with a bald head shaved clean except for a small braid at the back, walked towards her. He administered a small dose of medicine to her. She swallowed it in a single gulp.

"Where am I? Wh…how?"

"King Dyaus was riding out to meet the King of the nearby kingdom. He saw a shack and went to rest there, but he saw a dead body on the door. Two Mlecchas were also there. And you," the doctor replied.

She felt her stomach. It felt unnaturally light. It felt empty!

The doctor sighed.

"We couldn't save your baby. The Mlecchas forced themselves upon you. You were in no condition to have a safe delivery. I'm really sorry. I can't even imagine the pain."

Saying so, he left the room. That day, her entire life had been destroyed. Her husband, her house and her baby.

She went out to avenge herself. She learnt from some soldiers that the Mlecchas had escaped. She went out to find them, and in a local tavern, she found them.

She invited the one who twisted her arm to a room in the tavern, where she cut his genitals—with a serrated blade, gaining rust.

She then invited the second one and did the same to him.

Her next step was to pledge loyalty to the King who saved her. She was appointed a soldier in the Deva army under Dyaus. She gained the loyalty of Lord Devendra Dyaus and got promoted rapidly from a soldier to a platoon commander to a Marut until the death of Dyaus.

She cried so much in the first few years of service that the soldiers nicknamed her *Rodasi, she who cries,* and the name stuck. Almost nobody, apart from Dyaus and Indra, knew her real name. Shachi.

23

Brihaspati tried to rearrange the apparatus. It was made of a wire frame and looked like a replica of the weapon—a central stem, six arms, a crystal holder at the end, surrounded by three smaller arms. The frame would hold a crystal prism at the centre. Three pieces of metal would cover it. They would be connected by wires deep inside the arms to the central stem. The exact process was repeated in the other six prongs.

When a current was produced, the piece of metal would act as an electromagnet. This magnet would then affect the crystals. They would spin violently and produce electric currents, stunning, killing or even setting flame to the enemy.

It was a complicated weapon to use. For instance, the Vajra had to be held at a particular angle to minimise or maximise the "Lightning's" effects. All seven prongs couldn't be used at once.

There was a knock on the door.

"Come in," said Brihaspati.

Mitra entered and touched the rishi's feet. Brihaspati blessed him with a long life.

"Guru Brihaspati, have you managed to do something?"

The Vajra crystals had been thoroughly cleaned and shaped into prisms.

"Prince Mitra, Look at this," said Brihaspati. He rubbed a piece of amber against his silk waistband and held it to the back end of the central stem. Instantly, the crystals began to glow, a white ray of light was produced, and the crystals began to spin.

Brihaspati removed the amber, and the wires instantly returned to normal.

"Woah! That is seriously cool!" exclaimed Mitra.

Brihaspati smiled, then sighed.

"What happened, Guruji?" enquired Mitra.

"It reminds me of your father. I was a young man. I had fallen in love. Madly! There was this teacher at our Gurukul. She was the same age as me, and she used to teach young children. I fell in love at first sight. She initially did not like me, rejecting my advances, but then she fell in love with me, being the handsome man I wa…I am."

Mitra grinned. Brihaspati smiled.

"Anyways, I married her, and we were happy. I had even got a job at the King of Mohenjo-Daro's palace as the Head Priest."

Mohenjo-Daro was an ancient city built on the banks of the Sindhu. Originally called Manavdurg, it was believed by many to be the birthplace of Lord Manu, the saviour of mankind.

"The King, Chandra, coveted my wife, Tara. I pretended to ignore it, but he was getting on my nerves. Then, I was framed for the murder of a renowned scholar. The King blamed me and forced Tara to marry him. It was before my imprisonment that I had met Dyaus. He studied with me in the Gurukul. He made me break out of the prison. He took me to his friend, Lord Kshetrapaal, the Rudra then. The Bhutagana army was prepared, and a war was waged. Chandra was exiled, and Mohenjo-Daro was given to the Rudra. So, I got my Tara again."

"Where..." asked Mitra.

"Dead. She died. Many years ago."

His watery eyes were staring distractedly at the heavens.

"I'm sorry."

"That's all in the past," said Brihaspati dismissively with a wave of his hand. He wiped his eyes.

"The Vajra is now nearing completion. We must make a frame for it."

"Of course. What do I have to get?"

"Bone. Wood might work, but it rots. The crystals seem to make wood rot faster. A steel frame would be good, but it might electrocute the user. Of course, I can insulate the wires, but that would be both time-consuming and expensive."

"What would be best?"

"A combination of bone and steel."

"Leave it to me."

Brihaspati nodded. Just then, a soldier walked in.

"Lord Mitra! Lord Varuna has arrived. He requests an audience with you and Rishi Brihaspati."

Mitra exchanged glances with Brihaspati. It was a surprise.

"Allow him in."

A few moments later, he walked in. In his early thirties, Lord Varuna was dressed in a sea-green dhoti and a blue angavastra. His clean-shaven face added to the calm and gentle aura around him, like the sea that he was named after. He had a silver turquoise ring on the middle finger of his right hand.

A ceremonial noose, the symbol of Dharma, a sheathed sword and a quiver were tucked inside his waistband. Marks on his right arm and fingers pointed him out as a swordsman and an archer.

He went to Brihaspati and touched his feet.

"*Ayushman Bhavah,*" Brihaspati put his hand on Lord Varuna's head to bless him.

He then went to Mitra and embraced him.

"My brother!"

"It's been too long, my brother," replied Mitra, having teary eyes.

Brihaspati smiled at the brothers' reunion. But, by Varuna's unannounced entry and formal demeanour, it was clear that the purpose with which he came was a serious matter.

"The King sends his regards. He hopes you have accomplished the task you came to Persia for."

Mitra knew that Varuna was talking about both Prithvi's necklace and the Vajra.

"Yes, we have done it."

It was not a lie. Mitra had sent a few soldiers to the main city bazaar a few days back to get the necklace. As for the Vajra, the materials, methods and manuscripts had all been collected and stored, some in Brihaspati's mind.

"The King requires your assistance. The wicked Panis have stolen the Deva cattle. The King does not want to endanger

New Amaravati, and so wants the soldiers you have. That is, if you'll come."

"We'll come," said Mitra without hesitating.

"But…" said Brihaspati.

"Guru Brihaspati, we have everything. It's time to leave. Our thousand-strong security force can be used better than wasting away here."

Brihaspati contemplated it before finally nodding.

"Give the orders. We leave tomorrow."

24

Two weeks and three days later, Mitra-Varuna's troops had joined the Maruts west on the opposite banks of the river. Mehrgarh lay just a few metres away. The soldiers were arranged in the standard turtle phalanx formation called *Kurm Vyuha.*

"We attack at night."

Mitra, Varuna and Rodasi nodded.

The plan was that the main body of soldiers would act as a battering ram to break open the main gate. The Maruts would then ride into the city through a canal. They would cause a stampede by staring at the cattle and directing it towards the primary battle. At a signal, the Deva armies would swiftly retreat, and Pani soldiers would be crushed under the hooves of running zebus.

It was a complicated plan. A lot could go wrong.

Mitra entered the war room.

"Can I see the plans, Commander?" he asked Rodasi. She nodded and gave the board to him.

"This won't work," said Varuna from behind Mitra's shoulder.

"There is no other way," replied Rodasi.

All of them stared at the battle plans. Heavy infantry and an elite group of spies would be required for the mission.

"We have heavy infantry, Varuna," said Indra.

"I'm not talking about the heavy infantry. I'm talking about the spies. I don't think the Maruts are trained for espionage."

Seeing Rodasi's mouth opening, Varuna quickly added, "I'm not doubting your troops, Commander. I am simply implying the obvious. The Maruts are too heavily armed. They are meant to be shock troops, not espionage groups."

"We'll manage that, Lord Varuna," said Rodasi, venom in her eyes.

"It can't be done. Firstly, we don't have small boats. Secondly, the dam."

Mitra's fifteen-year-old son, Vashishth, was staring contemplatively at the map.

"Father," he said. "Has Guru Brihaspati succeeded in…?"

Except for Indra and Varuna, all were staring perplexedly at the young boy. They were the only ones who knew about the quest.

"Not now…"

"No, wait! I have a strategy!"

The young boy's fearsome intellect was praised by all who met him. He had mastered the ancient and practically-extinct language Tamil, as well as the commonly-spoken Sanskrit. He could talk fluently in Prakrit and Paishachi too. He knew battle strategies. But his real interests lay elsewhere in spirituality.

"What would happen when we put… uh… put… put that thing in water?"

Mitra had never thought of that. He didn't care.

"What?"

"Hypothetically, if we put... that in water, then the main components of water will get separated."

"Main components?"

All others in the war room were now getting thoroughly confused.

"Leave us," said Indra, watching Vashishth struggle to talk freely.

The men ushered out, quite like a herd of sheep.

"Wait!" Indra said to one of the soldiers. He turned back.

"Get Rajguru Brihaspati."

25

The Rudra's audience chamber in the Great Pillared Hall was located in the southern part of the Citadel in Mohenjo-Daro. It had been built under the guidance of the previous Rudra, Kshetrapaal.

A wooden dais occupied the centre of the hall. Behind it was a curtain which covered the door and wall to Rudra's private office.

Surrounding the dais were four sandstone sculptures. The hall itself was south-facing. On the western side were a rhinoceros and a water buffalo. On the east were an elephant and a tiger. Two ibex were carved at the base of the four-foot-high dais. A mat was spread for Rudra to sit on.

A horned crown was placed on the ground, meant to be worn by the Rudra for ceremonial occasions.

The office was an image of simplicity. And sadism. A neatly folded lion skin lay in a corner of a rectangular room of ten-by-ten feet. A cobra was lurking casually in the corner. Clay vials of poisons and acids were sitting precariously close to the edge of a wooden table.

A stone bed covered in fine deerskin could have used polishing and fining. Ash and blood were smeared on the walls. A skull was placed in the exact geographical centre of the room.

The current Rudra, Bhairav, was a practitioner of the occult. A tantric himself, he had contributed profoundly to the subject with his many treatises on yoga.

Right now, the tigerskin-clad Rudra was deeply engrossed in a yoga pose. His meditative trances were long, drawn-out and energising. One could almost feel the energy in the room where Bhairav was meditating.

Somebody knocked on the door. An angry Bhairav picked up his trident, then remembered. He had taken the vow of temporary non-violence. He placed the trident back and went to open the door.

It was Adinath. Adinath was one of the Bhutaganas who was not born into the tribe. He used to be a householder but had long given up the material plane. He wanted to pledge loyalty to Lord Shiva. So, he went to Kashi.

His life went from a householder to a hermit to a Yogi to an Aghori, and finally, he joined the Bhutaganas. As a Bhutagana, he had to forget all other identities and take on the name the Rudra chose for him.

"Lord Rudra, the Council requests an audience," said Adinath.

Bhairav frowned. The Bhutaganas were under the strict command of the Rudra. However, all major Bhutagana clans elected their head to represent the Council of Shiva.

It was always formed in wartime. So, its formation now, at this time, was not a good omen.

He briefly glanced at the planetary chart on the floor.

Mars and Saturn seem problematic, he thought.

Mars was identified as the planet of conflict and war: Saturn, the god of delayed beginnings.

Bhairav draped the lion skin over his right shoulder and under the left armpit, leaving one arm bare. He followed Adinath into the conference hall.

"The God of Gods, Lord Shiva's representative, Lord Rudra!" cried the doorman.

The assembled nobles bowed in reverence to the one selected by Lord Shiva himself.

Bhairav sat on the given platform. He wore the horned crown over his matted locks arranged in a neat bun.

"Sit down!" he ordered.

"What's the matter?"

All the nobles began to speak at once.

"QUIET!" Bhairav roared.

"Markandeya, you speak!"

Markandeya's father was an important priest of the clan. His son had been diagnosed with a chronic illness that lowered his lifespan to sixteen years.

Bhairav, however, in the boy's last years, had taken a liking to him. He could not let a dear companion and disciple die. So, he gave the boy Somaras, quite like defeating the God of Death himself.

This had also earned Bhairav the title of *Kalaantak, the Destroyer of Time and Death.*

The boy survived and was now twenty-five years old. He had even started practising asceticism from the Great Yogi, Lord Rudra himself.

"Lord Rudra, you have been found guilty of murder by subterfuge. Recent evidence in Bactria has confirmed that the Fifth Head of Brahma, Lord Dyaus, has been murdered by you!"

A collective gasp escaped the mouths of those assembled. All of them had been led to believe that Vritra's damming project had forced the council's formation.

Bhairav's expression continued to remain stoic. He had to resign. His training had led him to stay strong. He knew he had no choice but to exile himself.

"If Lord Bhairav goes, we go!"

The extremist followers of Bhairav broke the silence. They were masters of Tantra and Yoga. They acknowledged Bhairav as being born from the hair of Shiva himself. Such devotion inspired rebellions and revolutions.

These people were also some of the most important members of the Tribe. They doubled as shamans, exorcists, warriors and doctors in times of crisis.

"I banish myself. But first, I need to elect a successor."

Bhairav thought. Hardly anyone was capable of leading the Bhutaganas. They were deadly.

But, Bhairav knew of an equally angry, potential successor.

"Rise, brave Pashupati!"

A man of twenty stood up. He had powerful biceps and well-maintained six-packs. He wore a white dhoti, crimson sash and a saffron angavastra.

"Do you, O Pashupati, accept your position as the leader of the Bhutaganas?"

Pashupati, with moist eyes, roared.

"I DO!"

"Then there is no more to be done here by me. I renounce the world, as well as my position as the Rudra. I am going to Kashi. I renounce the palace and everything on my person, including my clothes."

Saying so, he removed the horned crown and went to Pashupati. He put the crown on his head and went to his private office. He removed the lion skin shawl. He pulled off his tiger skin skirt and was clad in just a saffron loincloth, the colour of celibacy.

He picked up the skull. It would double as a begging bowl. He removed his sandals and took the trident in both his hands. He held it reverentially to his metaphorical third eye, between his brows.

Finally, he was ready to leave. To go to Kashi—the City of The Supreme Light.

26

"No! No! Please, we'll die!"

A non-violent protest had begun near the dam's construction site on the Sarasvati. The protestors were primarily women. The men were forced to work as labourers.

"My King, even the labourers are protesting!" cried an alarmed Construction Site Overseer.

"Whip those corpses till they bleed. Then we'll see who works and who doesn't," said Vritra.

"And what about the women, my king?" enquired the General.

"Your pups can't fight women, General?"

The General nodded and went to signal his soldiers.

Vashishth's plan had been set in motion. The crystals and the electromagnet had been placed in the river. Six hours from now, the water would have evaporated. The entry point of the canal had been obstructed by a wooden dam, effectively turning it into a dam.

Water comprises two primary components: *praanvayu,* or the air of life, and *udaanvayu,* the air that floats.

Furthermore, udaanvayu could, hypothetically be used to make *vimanas.*

An electric current in the water, passed through two electrodes, would separate these from each other. They would then escape in the form of bubbles.

He had named the two electrodes as the 'Mitra-Varuna duality'.

Six hours later, Rodasi and fifteen Maruts quietly slipped into the city. It was nearly close to sunrise. However, they had no choice. The operation couldn't wait any longer.

Quietly treading through the stream-shaped puddle on the ground, they entered the city. The sluice gate had been open, so the men walked in unhindered.

Each Marut, including Rodasi, was armed with a shortened javelin, three daggers, a short sword, a battle axe and light leather armour.

Black dhotis, cloaks and stockings were worn. A black turban with an attached veil hid their faces. Secrecy was essential.

The electric source had been extracted half an hour back with the aid of a bamboo stick. A dove had been thrown in the puddle to check for the current.

As the Maruts were marching ahead, Sarama's nose began to twitch. Sensing a bark coming on, Rodasi bent down on one knee and patted her snout.

As she began to ease, she signalled two men to check the area ahead. They saw a large black wolf-like dog growling at a golden tabby. They shooed the canine away. Problem solved.

They continued and reached the back wall of the Citadel. The cow shed was directly in front of the wall. Judging from the stench, that is.

"One of you! Climb over and check for a potential escape route!" Rodasi whispered.

No sooner than she said this, a loud war horn was heard. The battle had begun!

A commotion was heard from inside by the soldier. The soldiers had woken up and were now rushing out to fight. Of course, it was not possible to tell just by sound. Rodasi's man climbed the wall and stretched his neck to look. He signalled with his hands for everyone to come.

Rodasi and the men scaled the wall. They walked on the eighteen-foot-wide wall for a few feet. They couldn't directly jump into the cowshed. It might scare them into attacking.

They jumped a few feet outside the shed. A bull turned to look at the noise.

"Hurry!" whispered Rodasi.

The soldiers quickly set to work. Since the guards were not there, the Maruts needed no secrecy. The now-empty barracks were directly in front of the shed. The soldiers opened the lock. The cows began marching out one by one. The Panis' existing three-thousand cattle and the five thousand of the Devas were all successfully led out. Two Maruts sneaked behind the herd and roared. They beat drums and blew whistles.

The noise did its work. The cattle in the back flew into a frenzy and butted those in front. All of a sudden, chaos prevailed. Rodasi hit a few heifers in the gut with her sword butt. They moved in the direction of the sword pommel.

Suddenly, out of her eye, she saw a Marut nearly getting trampled by one of the bulls.

"Vrishabh, look out!" she shouted and ran towards him.

The bull thought better of it and instead attacked the lady. The horn instantly pierced Rodasi's arm—the other one was in her chest.

A fountain of blood gushed out. Her sword fell to the ground. The right leg was trampled on by fifteen hundred pounds of beef.

Call it a miracle of the gods or sheer luck, the bull changed direction to join the rest of the herd, leaving the victim in the sand of the Mehrgarh Citadel.

27

A loud war horn resonated clearly outside the Mehrgarh fort. The armies of the Devendra swiftly broke formation and retreated, left and right.

The Pani general thought it was a tactic to surround the Pani armies. But before he could act on his suspicions, his standing ground shook. He turned back to look.

Holy Cow!

Retreat was impossible. In front was the river. On two sides were the Devas. Behind were the eight thousand cattle.

The cattle approached closer. Three stallions emerged from one of the streets when he thought he would die.

"*Hyah!*" shouted the youngest of the three riders.

The cattle in the front recognised the voice. It was the manager of the Deva cowsheds. They knew they were safe. They stopped. The others behind them were still trying to shove and butt their way through.

The other rider, Indra, rode to the back and thrashed the renegade cows. Seeing their companions treated this way, the other cattle stopped dead in their tracks.

"Devas, retreat!" ordered the King of The Devas, protecting his troops.

"No! No! Mercy! Please! Mercy!"

Hearing the cries of the soldiers, Indra smiled. He looked at the Asura General. He was trembling from head to foot.

"Get me your King and you shall be spared."

28

There was a loud knock on the door.

"Come in," answered Danu.

Danu was in her sixties. She was born into one of the economically better-off Asura merchant families and had married relatively late in life.

She shared her name with the Asura water goddess. According to legend, Danu was the goddess of water and her sons were supposed to be massive giants.

Even after the killing of her husband and her abduction and purchase in Mesopotamia, she did not lose hope and courage.

She was dressed in a black dhoti with pink and red flowers, a purple blouse, a turquoise sash and a brocade stole.

Vritra entered.

"Mother, with your blessings, the dam project has been going splendidly well."

She smiled wanly. Though she knew her son was wrong in taxing the peasants' waters, she supported him wholeheartedly because she also wanted him to rule.

"Back so soon?" she asked.

"I had to come back. And anyway, I only had to be there to crush the locals' rebellion."

"Now, where's my gift? Don't tell me you forgot!" she pouted.

Vritra chuckled mirthfully. She joined in. He hugged her.

"Now, what will you do next?" she asked.

"I'm planning to send some spies up north. I need to check on the Panis. Something tells me that the Northern Forts are at the risk of an attack."

Over the past few weeks, Vritra had united the Kalakeya Asura tribes under a standard banner. The unification was quick and bloodless.

"And what about Tripura?"

Tripura was the collective name of three cities founded near the dam's site on the Sindhu. The three Citadels were under the control of Vritra's able General Tarakaksh. His brothers, Kamalaksh and Vidyunmali, commanded the other two.

"Tripura is safe. I heard that Rudra resigned. Bhairav has gone to Kashi. And the new one seems powerless to me. The Bhutaganas are divided. Nearly a quarter have left for Kashi."

Danu nodded. That sounded good enough.

29

"So, what will it be? A quick beheading or slow torture and death?" Mitra asked the Deva king.

The Pani King, Parvata was handcuffed. He was kneeling, his royal turban on the ground, under Indra's shoe.

A Marut came running in.

"My King!"

He was holding the nearly lifeless body of Rodasi.

"What is it… No! Get her to the medic!" shouted Indra.

"Kill him!" He whispered, gesturing to Parvata before going after the Marut. Going after the unrequited love of his life.

He entered the temporary hospital quarters. The doctors were desperately searching for any injuries on the vital organs.

After about fifteen minutes of searching for wounds, the doctors turned to Indra.

"No major injuries on her vital organs, Great Devendra. However, she has lost some blood. Not a very substantial amount. She'll have some weakness in her body, though. Don't worry. She'll survive. The leather armour saved her from the damage."

Thanking the doctors, he went to Rodasi's bed. One doctor was trying to close the wounds. He smiled good-naturedly. Indra did not respond. He was too busy fretting for the life of his love.

Nearly an hour later, the doctor finished his work. Cleaning his hands and instruments, he said, "She'll regain consciousness in a while. When she does, spread this ointment on her wounds and give her these painkillers. Gods willing, she'll be fit as a fiddle in less than a month."

"Thank you," said a grateful Indra.

"Just doing my duty," said the doctor with a dismissive wave of his hand. He was a Pani and was not aware of Indra's identity.

Indra continued to stare at the regal, strong and beautiful face of Shachi.

Her eyes opened in the dimly lit hospital room. Her vision was blurry. She looked at the blurry black figure staring at her. She focused her eyes.

Lord Devendra!

"My Lord!" she whispered weakly.

"Shhhhhh… Don't talk. The doctor told me to rub this ointment on your wounds," he started applying the ointment to her wounds.

She winced slightly at the rough, masculine touch and the ointment's burning sensation. His hands lightly touched the wound on her arm. He applied it on her leg, where the hoof print's mark was still visible. He used it on the damage down her lung. She winced.

Indra looked at the expression on her face.

"Something troubles you?"

"No, my Lord. It's just that you're the King and..."

"The bravery you showed was beyond measure. The Maruts tell me that you managed to save all of them in your actions. Not a single Deva casualty from your side. For that, I'm grateful to you."

She was not good at taking compliments. She blushed and tried to say something, but no words came out. Finally, after having rubbed the ointment on every possible injury, he picked up a clay cup. It held a yellowish-orange potion.

"Here, drink this. It's a painkiller. It'll speed up the healing process and help you sleep."

He handed her the vessel and went out. She stared at his retreating figure and smiled ruefully.

30

It had been two months since Rodasi's bruises had been lovingly anointed with medicine. Since then, she and Indra had developed a friendship. They laughed, talked, discussed royal matters, gossiped about ministers, and even joked.

She had now begun to get up by herself and had almost completed the recovery process. However, she still required a stick to walk. She was elated at the prospect of being able to walk again. However, would she still receive the same care from the man she had grown to admire? This was the question troubling her.

Indra walked in, flanked by Queen Mother Prithvi and two fourteen-year-old young boys. The boys seemed lost. Indra was dressed in a green angavastra with blue peacock feathers on it. A turquoise dhoti looked nice with the overall colour combination of the outfit. The boys' heads were shaven. They had tears and were dressed in coarse, wrinkly white.

"Mother, this is Commander.... uh..."

"Shachi, Your Highness."

She preferred her older name without the connotation of grief.

"Pleased to make your acquaintance."

"Shachi, we have developed a good friendship over the past few days. Do you not think... we should... take it to the next stage... I mean, we... I..."

He took in a deep breath.

"Before the past two months, I admired you only as a warrior. Your fighting skill is irreplaceable. Your inner fire is the gift of Lord Agni. However, I never appreciated your beauty before. You shall make a fine Queen of The Devas. Will you, I mean..."

Prithvi was looking at her son. His embarrassment forced a smile on her face. Shachi, too, started giggling.

Her giggles further hurt his pride and confidence.

"I'm sorry. Please, carry on," she said, straightening up.

He cleared his throat.

"Will you marry me?"

He couldn't believe the voice coming out of his throat. The deep, booming baritone was replaced by a shrill treble, more like a teenager's, at the start of adolescence.

"But, you're the King and... why me? There are Apsaras far prettier than me."

The Apsaras were a tribe of wandering courtesans. Their enormous pleasure pools and water dances had led people to liken them to water nymphs.

"No one comes close to you."

These words were enough.

"Will you marry me?" he repeated.

The butterflies in her stomach were restricting her speech. She couldn't bring herself to answer. After what seemed like an eternity, she nodded.

The King of the Devas stared triumphantly at his to-be wife. For the first time in her presence, he was forced into silence.

Prithvi sensed the awkwardness in the room.

"Uh… son," she said, pointing towards the two boys.

"Oh, right!"

He followed his mother outside the room. He turned back to look one last time at Shachi before marching out.

31

The men were sitting in a circle around the fire. They were the loyal followers of the previous Rudra, Bhairav. Nearly two hundred had marched out of Mohenjo-Daro to stay with the beloved ascetic. They were in Ujjain. They had performed a yagna at the ancient site of the Mahakaal Shiva temple. Bhairav had bought a piece of land for his samadhi.

Thousands of years later, this place would be known as the Kaal Bhairav Temple. For now, however, the cremation ground where they sat would have to suffice. Bhairav wasn't going to die anytime soon.

The men were smoking from chillums and were drinking distilled liquor from goatskins.

Bhairav was slowly roasting a deer over the low campfire. Life was always good for Yogis, as it should be.

32

Indra was reading the ancient manuscripts from his father's private collection. These manuscripts contained a detailed history of the gods. The chapters in the beginning were dedicated to Lord Vishnu and his Avatars.

Lord Matsya was the first Avatar. In the flood during Lord Manu's time, the boat they were stranded in had become lost at one point. That was when, almost like a signal from the gods, a dolphin emerged and tugged at the rope hanging from the hull. Later inspection proved that this was the same fish Manu had saved some years back. Manu, a devout believer of Lord Vishnu, had proclaimed the fish as the First Avatar.

The second Avatar was Lord Kurma. The Devas and Asuras were gathered at Mount Mandar to search for the Amrit, a refined form of the Soma. However, underwater plants that were the core ingredient of the Amrit could not be found. A turtle was sent into the water to retrieve the plants. However, since turtles lived for two centuries, their blood, too, was required. The turtle was ritually sacrificed and proclaimed the second Avatar. The Asuras did not receive Amrit. The consort of the Rudra, Lord Neelkanth's wife Mohini, distracted the Asuras and gave them sweetened water, instead.

Lord Varaha was the third Avatar. He was a giant boar. Legend says the Asura Lord Hiranyaksh had attacked ice caps with incendiary weapons to flood the world. The then Devendra, Lord Suresh, duelled the Asura lord. Out of nowhere came this gigantic, hulking beast who gored Hiranya to death. The flood was conveniently stopped. Dams were built, and Vajras were placed in water.

Lord Narasimha was the next Avatar. His disfigured face, perfectly styled beard, and leonine mane made him appear like a lion. Hiranyaksh's brother, Hiranyakashyap, was the greatest Asura warrior. He defeated all the Devas. He had bodyguards that stood guard during the day, night, palace, and outside. However, there were six minutes when the day guards had gone to rest, and the night guards were still on their way. The doorway was unsafe. Narasimha ripped the King's chest to shreds with his adamantine metal claws, toppling a pillar on the guards inside and blocking the entrance of those outside.

Lord Vaman was a great Deva warrior. He defeated the Asura King Mahabali, a descendant of Hiranyakashyap. The Asuras were conquered and exiled to Pataal, an island south of Mesopotamia.

The Asura supremacy was over. The evil now faced by Sapta-Sindhu was that of Kshatriya supremacy.

The Sixth Avatar, Lord Parashu Ram, had rid the earth of the twenty-one major Kshatriya clans that had begun to oppress the Brahmins. Their dictator, Lord Kartavirya Sahasrabahu Arjun, had all been slaughtered like pigs with his five hundred bodyguards. Arjun had killed Parashu Ram's father, Jamadagni, with the same axe that would take his life.

The seventh Avatar, Lord Ramchandra. He was the ideal King, ideal son, ideal prince, ideal husband and ideal father. Just to make his stepmother Kaikeyi queen-mother of Ayodhya, he renounced the throne and agreed to a fourteen-year exile in the south of Aryavarta. In the thirteenth year, his wife, Lady Sita, was kidnapped by the Rakshas warlord Raavan with the aid of his flying machine, the Pushpak Vimana. Midway, Jataayu of the Garuda tribe rammed his own Vimana into Raavan's. The unfortunate Jataayu's Vimana had been damaged by Raavan's Vimana's armour plating and crashed into the Dandak forest. He was rescued from the wreckage and given water. However, he died just after telling Ram the direction and identity of Raavan. Ram waged a mighty war against Lanka with the help of the Vaanar army and killed Raavan. By the rules of the exile, he couldn't call upon Ayodhya for help. That was why he took the aid of mere tribals. His whole life was a reflection of the rules he abided by. He truly was Maryada Purushottam, the supreme rule follower.

In the next age, rules were meant to be broken. Lord Krishna, Leela Purushottam, the supreme game changer. He was a major supporter of the Pandavas in the Mahabharata war. He broke the rules to establish Dharma in Aryavarta before departing from the earth. At the same time, his brother emphasised renunciation. That was when the Asuras regained allies and attacked the Sapta-Sindhu. The weakened armies were quickly defeated, and the Devas were driven out.

Indra's thoughts were interrupted by a knock on the door.

33

It was the two boys, Nasatya and Dasra. Their father had recently expired in the Battle of Mehrgarh. He was the commander of the cavalry regiments. Prithvi took pity on the fatherless boys and their mother, Sanjana. Prithvi took them in and allowed them to live in the royal quarters. They were family.

"Lord Devendra, we—"

"I'm your elder brother. Not the King. No need to be formal," he smiled at the two boys.

The boys were still grieving. They were ashen-faced and were bearing a sword. He had given it to the boys to take to the smith for sharpening.

Indra inspected the sword. It was a scimitar. It belonged to Dyaus. It still bore his initials on the underside of the hilt.

"I, too, lost my father. I guess it's more difficult when you spend time with someone than just hearing his stories," he said.

The boys were staring at the ground, tears streaming down their cheeks.

Indra put his hands on their shoulders.

"We should leave," they said and exited.

Indra felt terrible for the boys.

34

Two years had passed since Vritra's dam construction in the south of Kurukshetra.

The Sarasvati was again dammed in some southern territories. Only a few cities under the control of the Kalakeya tribes were allowed to have water.

Vritra was sitting in the corner of his office. He was tending to the scar on his knee. He had recently sustained the injury while out hunting.

Tarakaksh walked in. He was a man of twenty with long, shoulder-length hair and horseshoe moustaches. He was dressed in a yellow angavastra and orange dhoti. A red turban proudly sat on his regal head. His eyes indicated an excellent sense of humour. However, his troubled expression suggested otherwise.

"My Lord, I carry disturbing news. The spy you sent to the Pani Citadel returned after six months. He carries news. The Devas have moved south and captured Mehrgarh. The Pani leader's head has been displayed outside the city gates."

"I knew it!" muttered Vritra. He should have acted on his suspicions earlier. The Northern Asura Tribes were the most vulnerable. The Northern Kalakeyas must be warned.

"Send a message to commander Vichitra. Tell him to

strengthen the defences of the city. One more thing! Tell our man to stay cautious. Those Brahmins may get suspicious."

"As you say, my king," saluted Tarakaksh.

Vritra stared into the distance.

Devas.

Pashupati was sitting in his office. He was the second Rudra with the name of Pashupati. Lord Pashupati I was the inventor of the famed weapon, the Pashupatastra, the missile of Pashupati.

The office previously occupied by Bhairav had been thoroughly cleaned. The poisons and potions were thrown away, the ash and blood wiped, and the inscribed yantras and mantras removed. They were replaced with official documents, scrolls, letters and the treaty with Vritra. The Sindhu too was dammed. However, Lord Shiva's and the Rudra's devotees outnumbered the two-million-strong army and could lead a revolt. After all, rituals in the Mohenjo-Daro Shiva temple required water. And nobody was going to take on the Bhutaganas in an all-out war.

That was why Mohenjo-Daro was the only kingdom with an independent water supply.

Pashupati was staring at the map on the wall. Tripura's location was at a strategic point on the Sindhu dam. The dam was built in the city of Tripura. The reservoir acted as a moat for the riverine fort. In an unusual design, the city was divided into three Citadels instead of a lower and middle city. An artificial hill was made in the centre. The three Citadels—

Gold, Silver and Iron— defended the hill. The three brothers, Tarakaksh, Kamalaksh and Vidyunmali, controlled each part of the city.

The fort proved to be in conflict with Mohenjo-Daro's water supply as more dams were built south of the main one at Tripura. So, a pact was made, and the Rudra's territories were given their rightful share of the waters. Political tension was at its peak.

35

The two boys were out riding with their elder brother, Indra. They had recently learned the art of hunting from their elder brother. Growing up in an environment where mounted warfare was the key to victory, the boys had, in keeping with tradition, been entrusted with their own horses at the age of four. Learning to ride from their father, the boys were well-versed in music, mathematics, medicine and navigation.

The boys' father, Savitar, was an *Ashwin.* It was an ancient title given to the Deva cavalry commander. Usually, there was only one Ashwin. However, exceptions existed. The most famous two-Ashwin pair was that of Lords Nakshatra and Divakshatra, who fathered the Pandava brothers Nakul and Sahadev.

Indra was confused over the election of the next Ashwin. Both the boys seemed talented enough to qualify for the post.

There's still time. They're too young, he reminded himself.

"Hey, boys! What have you got?" he shouted.

The two boys pulled the reins, and the horses trotted to Indra. Nasatya was carrying a leather bag stuffed with six dead hares and a deer carcass. Dasra held a long spear. Three fowl were impaled on the same shaft.

"That's enough for today," he smiled.

Two years had passed since Savitar's death. The boys, now sixteen, had focussed on honing their archery skills. To improve hand-eye coordination and the ability to shoot arrows in blurred vision, the boys often accompanied Indra to late-night hunts, which often stretched till daybreak.

"Let's move to the fort," he said.

The formal Deva capital still remained Amaravati. However, for all practical purposes, Mehrgarh was the capital. The tactical advantage of Amaravati was its structure. A single platoon could defend the city expertly and give hell to the invaders. Burning oil, flaming arrows, and Ballistas were used for the starting attack.

A rather unusual and destructive weapon used by specially trained Deva priests was the Agneyastra. A crossbow of sorts, the Agneyastra was named after Agni, the god of fire. Four feet in length, the crossbow was not the cause of dread. It was the projectiles.

Exactly four feet and two inches in length, the arrowheads were coated in a mixture of potassium and brimstone, which, when rubbed, sparked to produce a flame. After that, the archer had only three seconds to release the missile. The flame travelled up to reach a paper cylinder filled with a mixture of saltpetre, charcoal and brimstone. Huge flames, reaching the heavens, consumed everything in their path.

A complicated weapon and one of the last surviving Divyastras, a lot could go wrong in its use. Wind speed, direction, temperature, friction, and the flight path must be considered while shooting it. That was why it had never once been used in the past 280 years.

Even in the Kurukshetra war, it had been used sparingly.

36

Mehrgarh had decked up in all its glory. The people were preparing for the wedding of their beloved ruler, Indra.

The Devas had not witnessed such a grand-scale wedding since Dyaus' marriage to Prithvi. The city was decorated with elaborate white and blue ribbons. The fort's gates had been decorated with images celebrating the conquests and victories of the past Devas.

On the centre of the gate was a bronze sun, its rays streaming out in all directions. Murals of Lord Meghavahan, Lord Indra I, Dyaus, Lord Maghavan, Lord Parjanya, Lord Purandar, Lord Shakra and the other Great Devendras of the past paid homage to the rich cultural heritage of the Devas.

Inside the city, the pavements had bronze sheets hammered into geometrical patterns and circles. The front gate of the Citadel had two massive eight-foot sandalwood sculptures of elephants standing sentinel at the gate.

The sandalwood had been specially ordered from Southern Aryavarta, the Land of the Vaanars and the Rakshasas. The areas South of The Narmada paid annual revenue of thousands of gold *mudras* to the Asuras in return for a promise of no interference in the political matters of the south.

Right after entering, all visitors were greeted by five-foot tall black marble bulls standing outside the southern gate of the yagna hall. Any sculptor would have difficulty copying the exact anatomy of the bulls. The horns, eyes and snout were all perfect—the tails were exact copies of each other. Everything from the protruding ribs, forehead, and genitals had been perfectly sculpted. The bulls seemed ready to charge.

Apsaras, wandering courtesans unmatchable in beauty, welcomed the guests with rose and jasmine-scented water. They were dressed in extremely revealing bodices, translucent muslin, skirts pleated in the front and white stoles that barely covered anything. Gold belts, anklets and other jewels decorated them.

A yagna platform, the *vedi,* occupied the centre of the hall. The assembled Brahmins were waiting for the auspicious time slot, or *muhurta,* for the wedding. The wedding had been delayed by two years because of the inauspicious positions of the Moon, the God of Emotions; Mars, the God of War; and Saturn, the God of Delayed Beginnings.

Nearly half an hour before sunset, the muhurta of the yagna would commence, and the priests would light the sacrificial fire and chant hymns from the Vedas. None of the assembled guests thought that new hymns would be added half a century from today—hymns in praise of Indra, Mitra, Varuna and the Ashwin twins.

The ceremony was completed without fuss. The bride and groom were asked to walk seven steps together. These seven steps symbolised the masculine and feminine creative energies. It symbolised the activation of Chakras, the seven rays of the sun, the seven colours of the visible spectrum, the seven musical notes and the seven promises made by the groom and bride to each other.

Finally, the wedding was over, and the priests finished the yagna by chanting *Om shantih, shantih, shantih.*

Let there be peace, peace, peace.

37

The War Council was assembled in the Great Hall of Brahma, the ceremonial name of the laboratory of Lord Hiranyagarbha. The legend goes that it was right here in this very hall that the blueprints of a new civilisation were drawn. The blueprints were entrusted to the Saviour, Lord Manu.

The rebuilding of civilisation from scratch was tedious work. But Lord Manu was a charismatic leader who convinced people to do their duty, saying that the Deluge was gods' way of punishing the previous civilisation who shirked their duties.

Mohenjo-Daro was the Gandharva term for the city of Manu, as it was the place where Lord Manu and Lord Yama's fleet first saw land.

The hall's centre was occupied by a large, thick table made of ebony wood. A map was pinned on the table. General Shushna, The Chief Engineer, Prime Minister Chandan, Commander Vichitra of the Northern Kalakeyas, Nagaraja Takshak, and Vritra were trying to devise a strategy to regain Mehrgarh.

"Serves them right. Those Pani bastards haven't paid the taxes for six years. Now they're languishing in jails!" spat Prime Minister Chandan.

"I agree. The costs are too high, the army is tired, and the Shatadri dam is nowhere near completion," interjected General Shushna.

"But it'd be prosperous for us to help them! We could demand money from those fabulously wealthy oversized peacocks and get them out of there," said the Chief Engineer.

"And be called cowards?" thundered Chandan.

"Enough," said Vritra, banging his fist on the table.

Everyone fell silent.

"What is the more prosperous course of action, Prime Minister?"

"My Lord, both carry equal loss. The dam's protection will be lost if we redirect our army to Mehrgarh. And if we stay and the Panis regain power, they'll revolt. And if they don't, the Devas might regain their lost territories."

"Can we redirect more troops to the northern fortresses?"

"Well, we can, but…"

"Then we do it."

"And the Panis, my liege?"

Vritra picked up a quill and sketched a rough map of the Kalakeya empire. The map was accurate up until the area around the Bolan. He purposely left Mehrgarh and surrounding areas outside.

The gesture was clear. Mehrgarh was to be ignored.

No words were exchanged as Vritra handed the map to the minister.

"The council is dismissed!" he said, waving his hand dismissively. The assembled nobles stood up, saluted and exited. Vritra leaned back in his chair and sighed.

38

The King of the Devas sat with his Queen on the jewel-encrusted throne. Indra's expression was inscrutable. He had just received the news. Brihaspati had been assassinated. One of the Pani ministers had broken out of jail and started a riot. The Deva police tried to suppress the escapees, and the crossfire killed the Royal Priest.

"He was alive when I found him," croaked Varuna.

Mitra held the escaped minister by the scruff of his neck. His face had been bashed in a wall just enough times to not kill him.

Indra calmly descended down the throne. He held the man's throat and punched him in the face. Then he kneed him in the groin. The man staggered and fell back down. Indra kicked his Adam's apple repeatedly until the man drowned in his own blood and died.

"His last words were… were…" tears welled up as emotion choked Mitra. The beloved Guru, the only father figure he had ever known, had passed into a higher realm. The lump in his throat was making it difficult to say anything.

"He said, 'The Angiras will help the King. Tell them my name and ask for help,'" said Varuna, completing Mitra's sentence.

The frame for the Vajra had not yet been designed. Each

time Brihaspati tried to complete it, either the frame was damaged or the wires snapped.

"Did he say anything else?"

"He told me that teaching you was his life's honour. He said that in another life, he hoped that you would teach him."

Tears gushed out in a flood as Indra's knees failed. He staggered back and was prevented from falling back by Shachi. The Guru that built the foundations of his life and his empire was no more.

Hiranyastupa had just received a scroll from the King of The Devas. The news was shocking. His Guru and predecessor, Brihaspati, had expired in an unexpected riot. He had been promoted to the rank of Chief Angira. Though he wanted to become chief of the clan, he didn't want it this way.

He read on.

The King of The Devas requires an audience with me?!

The Angiras were one of the less important Brahmin clans. They didn't have much say in the political matters of Amaravati or the Aryavarta. However, their vast knowledge of local issues made them much respected among the Brahmin community.

He read on.

So, Guru Brihaspati told them about the Vajra.

"Ribhu! Get your brothers. We're leaving for Amaravati."

"When?" Ribhu asked Hiranyastupa. A man of twenty-nine, his rippling musculature intimidated the man, yet his eyes had a sense of calmness. A lifetime of working in a forge had brought callouses and burns on his hands.

Though traditionally, the Angiras were only priests, anyone talented enough could join the tribe. Since the members were sworn to celibacy, the tribe's continuation directly resulted from a competitive test.

Mostly, brahmins passed the test. However, understanding of the Vedas was the only parameter. So, some Kshatriyas, Vaishyas and Shudras also became Angira Brahmins.

Ribhu and his brothers, Vaja and Vibhu, were all blacksmiths with an incessant desire to study and achieve something. They mastered the Vedas with the help of their Guru and gave the test. They were qualified to become Brahmins.

Even after becoming Brahmins, they still forged weapons in their free time as a hobby.

"We're leaving now," said Hiranyastupa.

39

The men in the room sat on comfortable sofas in a circle. In the middle of the hall was placed a table. The only objects in the room were an oil lamp, a map, a few manuscripts, scrolls, and a leather pouch. Other than the furniture, of course.

Ribhu extended his arm to reach the pouch. Hiranyastupa slapped it and glared at him.

"Not now!" he hissed.

He was naturally curious and wanted to inspect the pouch. The outlines of hard metallic objects and stones could be seen from the fine cotton pouch.

The door opened, and Indra, Shachi, Mitra, and Varuna walked in. The assembled Brahmins stood up to receive the Deva King.

"Lord Hiranyastupa, my sincerest apologies for making you wait. I hope your journey was comfortable and pray we did not cause discomfort."

"Not at all, Lord Devendra. The carriages you provided might have spoiled us simple Brahmins," he smiled genially at the King of the Devas.

"Allow me to introduce my wife, Shachi, and my elder brothers, Lord Mitra and Lord Varuna."

Hiranyastupa folded his hands and greeted them.

"These are my students, Ribhu, Vibhu, Vaja, and this is Tvashtri," he said, pointing to the four craftsmen. Tvashtri's eyes widened in surprise. Adjusting his expression, he smiled, folded his hands into a namaste, and bowed his head.

Tvashtri was a man of nearly sixty. He had a wispy beard, and his head was shaven except for a small tuft of hair at the back. The tuft and a *janeu* marked him as a Brahmin. However, his tanned skin, battle scars and calloused arms made him a warrior. Still, his satchel, which contained a hammer with its handle sticking out, pointed him out as a craftsman.

Other than Brihaspati and Hiranyastupa, hardly anyone knew that Tvashtri was an excommunicated member of the Bhutaganas; a deserter from the Rudra's army. The stress and war experiences gave him nightmares. Then, he learned of the Angira library from a local traveller in a tavern. He read the free-of-cost scriptures, which provided him with some inner calm.

"Namaste," greeted Indra.

"May all the gods of our great land continue to bless you, Great Devendra."

Mitra signalled with his eyes.

Show-off!

Varuna signalled him to stop it.

"May they bless us all, Tvashtri ji," added Shachi.

"Let us take our seats. These knees are not what they used to be," smiled Hiranyastupa.

Two aides came in and served the drinks. Since Brahmins abstained from alcohol, the wine had been replaced with iced and sweetened lemon juice.

Hiranyastupa politely declined. Tvashtri, Ribhu and Vibhu each picked up a goblet. Vaja gulped it down in one sip.

"The Deva guest house is for your use only. You may contact us anytime. We shall talk more tomorrow," said Indra.

Hiranyastupa nodded. Then he folded his hands into a namaste and walked out.

After they left, Mitra turned to Indra.

"Bhikshuk seems untrustworthy."

"Bhikshuk?" asked a puzzled Indra.

"That Tvashtri!"

Indra laughed at his brother's joke. Bhikshuk meant beggar.

"No, seriously!"

"It's nothing. They are friends. Guruji trusted them."

"Still, I have a bad feeling," said Mitra darkly.

"Oh, relax!" said Varuna, slapping Mitra on his shoulder. Mitra playfully retorted by punching his chest. Varuna staggered and fell to the ground, making groaning sounds.

Mitra and Indra burst out laughing. Varuna, too, stood up and joined in. Life was as good as it should be.

40

Lord Surya, the Sun God, started his day early in Bactria. Nearly one hundred Deva priests had gathered to pay homage to the nourishing, life-giving god. It was, after all, the day of the Sun—the first day of a new week, a new journey across time. At the exact moment of sunrise, they performed an *agnihotra* fire sacrifice, followed by ceremonially offering water to God.

"Om Suryaya Namah," whispered Hiranyastupa, paying obeisance to the God of The Sun.

He had already completed his morning rites from his chamber and joined his students in Indra's chamber.

Indra walked in a few moments later and bowed to touch Hiranyastupa and Tvashtri's feet.

Ribhu and his brothers were younger, so Indra didn't touch their feet.

"So, Lord Devendra—"

"Just Indra, please. You're embarrassing me. You're older. You're just like my teacher."

Hiranyastupa smiled.

Maharishi Brihaspati has taught him well! Seems like half the battle is won, he thought.

"You're the King of the Devas."

"And you're a Brahmin, the preserver of knowledge."

Hiranyastupa smiled.

"All right, Lord Indra. Let's get straight to the point. We know that Lord Brihaspati told you of the Vajra. We can construct it. It's not that difficult. However, that knowledge is privy to a select few. Even Lord Brihaspati did not have that knowledge. Tvashtri and Ribhu know it. They have read the scriptures on the Divyastras."

Indra stared hard at the leather pouch on the table, which contained the crystals and the magnets.

"I want a test."

"Test?"

"I want to test which craftsman can produce a divine weapon."

Hiranyastupa smiled in admiration at the King who would become a god.

Lord Brihaspati was right. The man will serve our cause.

"We can organise the test whenever you wish, great King."

"Lord Hiranyastupa, if the men are free, may I arrange it today?"

"But, of course! Tell them to meet me in the forge after lunch."

"As you wish," said Hiranyastupa.

The three brothers and Tvashtri were gathered in the forge. Three hearths had been kept in three corners. Judging from the burnt charcoal marks, the fourth hearth had been removed. The challenge had been knowingly made difficult. Metal parts, wooden beams, ropes, poles, spears, whittling knives, saws, hammers and many other tools had been kept neatly in the centre of the room.

Indra entered the room.

"Good afternoon. As you can see, there are three hearths and four of you. That is why either two of you team up. Or, one of you does without a forge. The challenge is to make a catapult or similar long-range weapon. You will have two days to do so. Good luck!"

Saying so, Indra exited the forge.

"So, what do we do?" asked Vaja.

"You three use the forges. I'm going to make something different. Without a forge," said Tvashtri.

One day had passed since the challenge commenced. Contrary to what Indra had expected, Ribhu and his brothers did not team up against Tvashtri and designed their own weapons instead.

The three designs of the brothers seemed nearly identical. Ladle-shaped catapults that worked by leverage. Since Tvashtri did not have a forge, he chose wood as the material to work with. In just one day, he had finished the bow part of a crossbow that was even bigger than the Agneyastra.

Right after his prayers, Tvashtri set to work the following day. A wooden rod was smoothened, sanded and cut to length. Tvashtri carved a groove into the surface and placed it on the table. He then picked up a wooden beam, measured it and cut it to length. The projectile was nearly complete. Nearly.

"My King, may I request a favour? The weapon that I am designing requires combustion and an explosion. I need some saltpetre, brimstone and a paper cylinder."

Indra stared quizzically at the craftsman, for these were the same ingredients used in the Agneyastra.

"I'll get them," he said before marching out.

Tvashtri resumed his work. A few moments later, Indra walked in with the powder for the Agneyastra, glue and paper. He noticed the broken glass and metal shards on the table.

"What have you done to the windows?" he asked.

Tvashtri chuckled.

"Patience, my king, patience," he said while rolling the paper leisurely. He then carefully placed the iron shards and sharp glass pieces inside so as not to damage the cylinder. The flammable adhesive was applied to the paper, and the cylinder was attached to the projectile shaft.

"BEHOLD!" roared Tvashtri.

The three brothers paused.

"THE INDRASTRA!"

41

"I still think you should go," pleaded Vritra.

Vritra and Danu sat alone in the dining hall of the palace. Vritra had suggested sending Danu to Tripura. It was considered the safest fort in the Sapta-Sindhu.

There were rumours that the Devas, his spy said, were mobilising. The Angiras had pledged loyalty to the Devendra, Indra. An age-old belief had been sparked.

The Asura ideology of racial purity had been the reason they were hated, and Vritra was a patron of the ideas of racial purity.

There were rumours with evidence that thousands of years ago, to maintain the purity of the bloodline, incest had been quite popular among the nobility.

The hatred for Devas was nothing but unreasonable, racial, and unjustified, meant to appease the nobility.

"But why? No harm here. The Devas are nowhere near the capital."

"But if a siege was triggered, not just by the Devas, but even the Nagas or the peasants, then I can't risk anything happening to you."

"And you'll stay here?"

"The fort is well-defended. Still, safety measures."

"All right. I shall leave tomorrow at noon," said Danu.

"The Indrastra?"

Indra had never heard of such a weapon before. The previous Devendras were famous for owning flaming arrows, the poisoned javelin Vasavi Shakti, and the Vajra.

Tvashtri elaborated.

"Named after your ancestor, Lord Indra I, the Indrastra is similar to the Agneyastra except for the effects. While the Agneyastra is a fire bomb, the Indrastra releases sharp metallic shards on impact. Almost as if divides into multiple missiles from one," said Tvashtri with a sly grin.

"Does it work?"

"Oh hell, it does!"

"Can we try it on the battlefield? Now?" asked an eager Indra.

"No, no. Hold on. The Indrastra is accurate from only a high platform. Maybe an elephant or something."

Indra fell into contemplation.

"Can we shoot it from the bastions to the riverbank? We can even place wooden statues of soldiers and test the range and accuracy, too!" said Indra.

"That sounds great! Shall we try it, or do you want to look at Ribhu and his brothers?"

Indra glanced at the three brothers. They wore the same sheepish grin on their face. It was outsmarted by an old man with feeble knees who wasn't even using fire.

The Ribhu brothers had made three prototypes of actual war weapons. The three "ladles", as they called them, were used by the Angiras to defend their city.

"Lord Ribhu, we can install full-size replicas of these weapons outside city gates," said Indra.

Ribhu smiled. He and his brothers had lost. However, Indra was not going to disappoint them.

He's a good man.

"That's too kind of you, Your Highness."

The three weapons resembled spoons mounted on wheeled stands and working on the leverage principle.

"Shall we test the weapon?" asked Tvashtri impatiently.

"Yes, yes. Come on. Lead the way," said Indra.

A platform had been erected to keep the bow stable. The butt of the bow was carefully placed over Tvashtri's shoulder. The projectile was ready. Only a spark was needed.

"My Lord," said Tvashtri.

Indra picked up the flint and rubbed it with his dagger. A tiny spark was seen, but not enough to set the arrow on flame. And then another. The potassium hissed and caught fire. Tvashtri nearly fell off balance but managed to shoot the arrow before the explosion. It soared for less than three seconds, and "BOOM!"

The arrowhead exploded in mid-air, and out flew chunks of metal and shards of glass. The shrapnel pierced the straw dummies. The soldiers would have been running away helter-skelter if it was an actual regiment. Most of the glass shards were too small to be seen by the naked eye. The size also meant thicker blood vessels could be blocked and cut, and the gods know what else.

"YES! AHA! YOU'RE A GENIUS, TVASHTRI!" roared Indra. A few shepherds gazed up to see the ecstatic King dance over the main bastion.

Controlling himself, he asked, "Can you mass produce these, Tvashtri? Also, I want you and ONLY you to build my Vajra. When can you start?"

"Today itself, if you so wish, Lord Devendra," said an overjoyed Tvashtri.

"Then get to work."

Tvashtri couldn't control his excitement. He fell on his knees and thanked the Sun God.

"May Lord Surya bless you, Great Devendra."

An embarrassed Indra turned his face away and pretended to examine the crossbow.

"My Lord, a scroll has arrived from our man. He says that the mission is complete. The nobles trust him completely," said the attendant.

"Good," said Vritra.

The Angiras had a traitor amongst them.

"And the Devas?"

"No signs of activity yet, My Lord. No mass army movements. I think they've stopped at Mehrgarh. Or maybe they don't want to move inward."

"Are they weak?"

"No weakness was reported. Although the Ribhus are with them."

"DAMN!" cursed Vritra.

The Ribhus made the finest chariots and war machines. The Angiras controlled them but had no idea how advantageous they would be. However, the new Deva leader, Indra, was an extremely cautious and intelligent man. The Ribhus' war machines could be put to good use by him.

"And the Bhutaganas?"

"Reports say that the Rudra is out of Mohenjo-Daro. Though, the sources are unreliable."

Vritra nodded.

"Is that all?"

"Yes, my king."

"Then go. You're dismissed. And prepare mother's carriage. She leaves for Tripura today."

The attendant bowed and left. Vritra looked at the map on the wall. He couldn't let those fair-skinned foreigners defeat the land's original inhabitants.

42

Indra and Hiranyastupa were gathered around a campfire. They were watching twigs being devoured by the flames. Indra was staring contemplatively.

"Lord Agni purifies everything he touches."

Indra nodded.

"Did you know that Lord Agni was an actual person? He was the first chief of a small clan of Brahmins who would later be called the Angiras."

"I never knew that," answered Indra.

"Yes. Sometimes, philosophy and faith clouds reason and rational understanding. But that doesn't mean Lord Agni was just a mortal, not the God of Fire. His inner fire, the warrior spirit, was why he is the God of Fire."

Indra smiled at the simple truth, conveyed meaningfully and simply. So simple, yet so profound.

The Angira moved to the point—the reason he actually came here.

"Lord Brihaspati believed that you were meant for greater things. That you had a purpose. He always talked in metaphors, and, to be frank, I couldn't understand most of them. Now, however, I have realised it. You are meant to save the Sapta-Sindhu from Asura tyranny."

Indra stared in surprise at the wizened old man.

"I'm sorry, what? I don't even live there! How can I defeat the Asura empire? I heard that the Kalakeyas have united. I'm sorry. My army can't go that far."

Hiranyastupa stared apologetically at Indra.

"The people in the Sapta-Sindhu are desperate. They need a new leader. The Asura empire must go. Do you know that Vritra has stopped the rivers? Ten thousand miles of forests have been cut to accommodate roads, Citadels and wood for the dams. The rains haven't fallen once since he ascended the throne. And you know who the people turn to for the rain."

Lord Indra I, the first Devendra. The god of rain and thunder.

The legend goes that the first Devendra, Lord Indra, pierced the primordial cloud, causing the rains to follow.

Hiranyastupa continued.

"Throughout the ages, the Asuras' ideology has been responsible for chaos and destruction. The Devas are looked upon as gods. If the entire Sapta-Sindhu comes under Asura dominion, neither Amaravati nor the Devas will be able to survive."

"Please excuse me," said Indra, barely controlling his anger.

This old man dares to tell the King of The Devas!

He stormed into the palace, glancing back one last time to look at the campfire. The flames seemed to flutter in the wind, almost as if they were trying to tell him something.

Indra gently opened his eyes. He was sitting at the same campfire from where he had just gone. Or had it been hours? By looking at the redness, he could judge that the Dawn Goddess was in the process of making a rangoli (colourful floral design) in the sky in honour of her brother, the Mighty Warrior, the Sun God.

Indra was just about to shout at Hiranyastupa when he saw he wasn't there. Somebody else was sitting in the same place where Hiranyastupa had been.

The man looked forty years old. His trefoil-patterned robe went from his right armpit to his left shoulder and hung loose from the arm. A gold headband, armband and chain were the only pieces of jewellery he wore. He looked unnaturally tall, even for a Deva, who commonly reached six feet and his shoulder-length hair was left loose. His greying beard, glowing visage, and muscular arms had a certain charm to them.

However, his large, limpid, almond-shaped eyes; rather than his face and muscles, attracted Indra. They were exactly the same as his! And even though Indra had never seen this man before, he automatically knew who it was.

"Father," said Indra with tears in his eyes.

"You've grown well," said Dyaus.

"Father…"

"I never expected this kind of weakling behaviour from you. I tried my best to break the Asura reign. I stole the Vajra, and I tried to acquire the Soma. I risked discovery and death. And I was the one betrayed."

"Betrayed?"

"Ask Hiranyastupa."

"Wha…but ho… You're just a dream! How do you know this?"

Dyaus did not answer. He was suddenly interested in the pendant hanging from his gold chain. It was a swan with a lotus in its beak—the symbol of Brahma.

"But, the Sapta-Sindhu…"

"It's your ancestral homeland. You were born there."

Seeing the puzzled expression, he added.

"Prithvi went to immerse my ashes in the Sarasvati. You were born at that time."

"It sounds hard to believe, but I, too, hold a grudge with the Asuras. Ask Hiranyastupa."

Dyaus suddenly began to turn blue. It's not regular blue, but an electric sort of blue. He began to disintegrate into blocks.

"NO! NO! FATHER, STAY! NO!"

"I never went anywhere, my son. I was always there; I shall always be there. For I am the sky!" Dyaus said, flying away with the wind. The wind brought the disintegrated pieces together and arranged them like a cloud—a cloud shaped like a bull.

"NO! NO! FAT-"

Indra woke up with a start. He quickly looked around. Nobody was there. The light of the full moon dimly lighted the room. It was clearly after midnight, judging by Ursa Major's position. That would mean four hours had elapsed since the argument with Hiranyastupa.

Indra did what comforted him best. He went on his knees and cried. He cried for the life he could never live. The life he could not enjoy. The life that was snatched away from him.

I shall avenge you, Father! Even if I must separate the sky and the earth, I shall do it! I swear on my blood. On your blood. On the blood of our ancestors. I SHALL KILL ALL OF THOSE BASTARDS AND DRINK THEIR BLOOD! THEIR WIDOWS SHALL GROVEL AT MY FEET! THE HEADS OF THEIR ORPHANS SMASHED IN THE WALLS OF YOUR TEMPLE! BY ALL THE GODS, THE ASURAS SHALL NEVER BE SEEN AGAIN!

"This is my oath. The oath of Indra," he whispered.

43

Early in the morning, Indra went to the river and bathed. Usually, the Devas had wells or Great Baths constructed for ablutionary purposes. However, Indra wanted to be away from the hustle of Mehrgarh.

The Panis who were willing to mend their ways had been allowed to retain their old homes used for Deva accommodation. Seeing the honourable Devas giving up their homes to the old inhabitants, those in the jails promised to mend their ways. So, an additional two hundred Devas had been welcomed into the clan.

After bathing, Indra quickly wiped his body clean with the towel and started getting dressed. A neatly folded silk dhoti was unfolded, making the two sides equidistant. Tying a knot, he took one of the portions and passed it through his legs. Making the pleats, he tucked the end inside the dhoti. The other side was pleated, too and tucked in the front. A crimson sash held it all together while completing the look.

Indra then picked up the shawl and draped it from the right armpit to the left shoulder. This allowed ease of movement of the right arm and protected the chest from the cold winds.

Finally, he wore the sandals and walked away from the river. He went to find out the man to whom he owed an apology. He went straight to the guest house library. The librarian, a thin, dusky man of forty, was busy reading a romantic play and did not notice, nor did bother to notice, the man who had just entered.

Do I look weird without a crown? No, wait! This is no time for jokes! Focus!

He looked around and saw a familiar old man reading an ancient war manual in a corner.

Indra rushed to the man.

"Lord Hiranyastupa," began Indra.

"Oh, Lord Devendra! What a pleasure to see you! I was just reading this fascinating manuscript! How may I have the pleasure of assisting you?"

"Lord Hiranyastupa, I... I'm sorry for my disgusting behaviour yesterday. I hope you'll forgive me. I should not have been so rude. I apologise."

Hiranyastupa smiled.

"Happens to the best of us, dear king. And you're a Kshatriya. Nonsense is intolerable to you, oh Great Warrior."

"No. I realise now that was cowardice. We must save my motherland. Our motherland."

"I have just one question for you, Hiranyastupa ji."

"Go on."

"I wanted to ask... I mean, if you know...It's related to my father, but... I mean... Guru Brihaspati..."

"I was his right-hand man, my Lord."

"Did he have any connections with the Asuras?"

Straight to the point, thought Hiranyastupa.

"All right, listen," he lowered his voice to a mere whisper. "We think that an Asura betrayed your father."

"What?"

"Shh. We think an Asura extracted a boon from the then-Rudra, Bhairav, to assassinate Dyaus."

If a fervent devotee pleased the Rudra with his devotion, then he was bound to grant the one greatest wish of that man.

"Which Asura?" asked Indra, the fire of fury blazing in his eyes.

The Angira leaned in closer.

44

The Asura woke up in the soft bed. He yawned loudly and scratched his navel. His wiry chest hair and the matted locks in his armpit were enough to make a child vomit.

Fort commander Vangrida was not the fittest army commander. For one, his large paunch did not allow him to see much below the centre of his navel. An asthmatic from childhood, weed-smoking in his teens meant he would get tired by the slightest bit of exercise. Heavy swearing, alcohol abuse, betel-stained teeth and smelly mouth added to the unpleasantness around him. Hair emerged from his ears, and sweat stank even a few feet away from him. His legs were hairy and hard, almost like beef with cactus spines.

However, he was fabulously wealthy and owned many slaves. His inheritance, which included Lakhan-jo-Daro, made him the Chief Kalakeya of the region.

His wife was thirty years younger than him. Married at eight, she was now a stunningly beautiful lady of twenty-one. Vangrida and his wife, Sunetra, even had three children. Not satisfied with one wife, Vangrida, a lustful man, had married three more women besides Sunetra and even had six concubines.

Satisfied with his life, he did not need anything more.

Nearly three decades back, he had saved Rudra's life during a hunt. A tiger had wounded him. Vangrida, passing through the forest, calculated his benefit and helped the Rudra. The simplistic Bhairav had offered a boon to him.

The grudge against Dyaus was an old one. The chief of the Devas, Dyaus, had control over the Dhatura plants and the Soma. Dyaus turned down the offer without wanting to trade with the Kalakeya chief. Vangrida, a vengeful man, vowed to have his revenge.

The opportunity presented itself with the Soma's theft by Dyaus.

If he couldn't be immortal, no one could be.

45

The twins were out riding. It was hard to see from such a distance, but it looked as if a party of a dozen men were tormenting a hermit on the ground. The boys, though still sixteen, had mastered archery and swordsmanship. They just couldn't let an innocent man die.

"You stay here. I'll go. At the first sign of trouble, shoot."

Dasra nodded.

Nasatya kicked his horse and rode up to the men.

"Salutations, my brothers. What brings you to these parts?"

Shit!

The men were wearing the black onyx pendant of the Kalakeya tribe.

"Who'd ya think ye are? Comin' up to us like that?" asked the fattest man, obviously the leader. The accent carried the lilt of the South.

"I mean no harm. My brother and I are just simple Mlecchas with no home to go to. Let us be. I was wondering if we could share a drink with you."

The man eyed him suspiciously. The man did not believe him. The boy wasn't even an adult. However, the scars showed a lifetime of combat.

"Arh! Sharin' a drink! Go away! Go back to yer mommy! And tell 'er the Kalakeyas send their love!"

The men collapsed in peals of laughter. Nasatya took in a deep breath.

"Who is this? Looks weak," he said.

"This lil' shit tried to assassinate me."

Nasatya stared at the frail man on the ground. He looked extremely old. His wizened face missed a few teeth and hair. A dagger was kept close to his hand on the floor. The bruises from the fresh assault gleamed scarlet against his brown skin. Wrinkled skin and protruding ribs added to the sense of weakness around him.

Yet, he had the nerve to try to assault the taller, younger and more energetic man, who, Nasatya thought, could knock the wind out of him in one punch.

"This…"

He pretended to smirk and laugh. The man lowered his eyes and stared at the ground.

"Stop laughing!"

Nasatya fell silent.

"Ya think this is a joke? This… This piece o' mud tried to kill me! The Chief of The Northern Kalakeyas!" the man barked.

Nasatya controlled his expressions. But it was evident that this was troubling news.

"Damn!" he said.

"We must kill him, Chief! So, how can we increase his agony? Let's see. Should we nail 'im to a wooden board an' ram a sword through his gut?"

"QUIET, YOU FOOL! I'LL DECIDE! YOU!" he turned to Nasatya.

"You're a Mleccha, aren't you? Paid mercenary barbarian, eh? Kill him for me. Then we'll share a drink."

"I'll… I'll just get my s-sword," muttered Nasatya.

"There'll be no need for that. Here," he handed him an axe.

Nasatya took the axe, his hands trembling. He turned to Dasra standing in the distance and nodded. Dasra nocked an arrow and fired in the direction of the leader. The Chief Kalakeya was shot straight in the neck.

The unorganised Kalakeyas were known to retreat if the leader died. However, the complete opposite happened. The other Asuras took out their swords. Nasatya swung the axe and decapitated one. He then slashed viciously and embedded the sword in another's skull. He took out his own sword, concealed by the cloak and beheaded another in a clean strike. Two arrows flew out in rapid suspension, and two were pinned to the ground.

The other seven tried to surround Nasatya but were all felled by the arrows of Dasra and the sword of Nasatya. Finally, there was only one surviving. He had thrown down his own axe and raised his arms in surrender.

"Spare me! Spare Me! PLEASE!"

"Where are you encamped?" enquired Nasatya calmly.

"I-I… We are encamped… en-encamped in…in … Lakhanjo Daro," the traitor said.

Dasra looked at Nasatya, and Nasatya nodded. In one clean stroke, the man was beheaded, and blood began to seep into a puddle.

"Well, now we know where to attack," said Dasra.

Lakhanjo Daro. The city of Lakshman.

Nasatya did not say anything. He was staring at the courageous man who was lying in the soil.

"Water...water! Please!"

Dasra pulled out his waterskin and offered it to the man. The man drank a few sips and tried to sit up.

"They...they killed my wife, my children. Decades before that, my parents, too, were killed by them. They burnt my fields and took my cattle. I... I tried to stop them, but I couldn't. I found him in a local tavern and attacked him with a kitchen knife."

"Shh. It's all right."

A sword had been brutally rammed through his gut. He only had a few minutes.

"NO! LISTEN!"

The boys stared in bewilderment.

"I...I know you're Devas. You're... Indra's brothers. I...I am Dadhyanch. I am... I know the location of the last reservoirs of Somalata."

Nasatya's eyes widened. He had just overheard Mitra and Varuna talking to Indra about the Somaras, the Soma juice.

"Where?"

Dadhyanch pointed to the place before finally succumbing to his injuries.

"Nasatya, we're too far away from home now!" said Dasra urgently.

"Quiet!" whispered Nasatya.

Dadhyanch had revealed the location of the last wild Soma reservoirs on the planet. He had pointed to a cavern that was concealed in plain sight.

The mountaintop was covered with trees. It was one of these trees that blocked the entrance of the cavern. To enter, one had to pass around the tree and squeeze in. Only adolescents or thin women could do it.

The cavern was completely dark inside. On top of that, it was spine-chillingly cold.

"Can we at least light a torch?"

Nasatya reluctantly agreed. He pulled out his knife and went out to search for a flint. Dasra followed him outside, taking care not to tread on something. Fear gripped his dehydrated throat as he saw a rider mounted on a chestnut stallion.

The masked rider was clad in a full-sleeved black tunic, reaching to his knees. A woollen black dhoti and shawl kept him warm. He was inspecting the corpses of the Fallen Kalakeyas.

"Hide, Dasra. I'll try to shoot him," ordered Nasatya.

Dasra went into the cavern with his head out.

Nasatya nocked an arrow and shot it straight at the rider. However, the man would have been dead if it weren't for the wind. The arrow whizzed past the man's ear, and he looked in its direction.

Nasatya nocked another arrow when the man removed his mask.

Oh, damn!

It was Mitra, the Slayer of the Bull.

46

"You guys have any idea how long you've been gone?" asked Mitra.

The boys had set up a campfire at the hilltop and were being scolded by Mitra.

"But… but Lord Mitra, we…"

"Brother," he corrected.

"Yes, Brother, we are searching for Soma!"

Mitra sighed.

"It's extinct."

"What? No. We met a man called Dadhyanch. We rescued him from the Kalakeyas. He said he knew the King. He… he said that the Soma is in this cavern!"

"Wait…what did you say his name was?"

"Dadhyanch," said the boys.

Mitra's expression changed to shock and then to realisation.

"Of course. Dadhyanch."

In one of Dyaus' letters, he mentioned someone called Dadhyanch.

"Did you get the Soma?" he eagerly asked the boys.

Nasatya shook his head.

"Take a torch, go into the cavern and search for it. Guru Brihaspati said it looked a bit like a leafless, budded vine with tuberous roots," said Mitra, barely able to control his excitement.

Nasatya picked up the torch he was trying to make earlier, set it on fire and squeezed inside.

Immortality lay just a few feet away in the darkness of the empty cavern behind Dasra.

A stone cup and a granite pestle lay on the ground. The fire was roaring against the stillness of the night. The Somaras were being prepared as per the proper rules and regulations.

As required, hymns to the old gods, the Soma itself, and the pestle were to be sung. This was the first step, the crushing of the plant.

After this, the Soma would be mixed with water and milk to remove the bitterness. However, it was still poisonous. That was why Dhatura was needed—preferably wild Dhatura from a specific northern strain.

Mitra racked his brains hard to remember the hymn to the pestle.

Dammit! I'm just going to leave it to the priests.

"We're going. Did you collect as much as you could?" he asked Nasatya.

Nasatya nodded. Dasra was staring at the vines.

"Let's leave," he repeated.

Dasra looked up and nodded.

47

"No. Bloody. Way!" said Indra.

"Yes, it's right here!" said Mitra, eyes shining with delight.

Varuna, Indra and Hiranyastupa were woken up two hours before sunrise for a private conference. The tired twins had been asked to go to sleep by a thoughtful Varuna.

"Who was the man?"

"Someone called Dadhyanch. The twins tell me he was killed," shrugged Mitra.

Hiranyastupa sighed. A tear escaped his eye. His back involuntarily slouched.

"Hey, what's wrong?"

"He used to be one of the Angiras. We used to study side-by-side. He was actually from the Prajapati tribe but passed the Angira test. He always wanted the Asuras exiled and defeated, as his own parents were killed by the Asuras. He was an extremely dear friend."

Indra put his arm on his shoulder.

Hiranyastupa wiped his tears.

"We'll take revenge for his soul," comforted Indra.

Hiranyastupa nodded.

"I swear on Lord Agni," said Indra.

He is the one, thought Hiranyastupa, not for the first time.

"Thunder and immortality. Doesn't sound like a bad combination," said Shachi.

"Oh, come on. If I get it, you and the Devas get it."

"Oh, caring for the public, are we?" she mocked.

Indra chuckled.

"You know, you're the only person who can say that and stay alive."

"Not even our son?"

"What son?"

It took Indra a moment to notice Shachi's bloated belly.

"By the gods! And you didn't tell me that before? Am I your husband or a damn handmaiden?"

She laughed.

"For me, you're just a slave meant to do my bidding, 'Your Highness'," she said teasingly.

"Wait, how are you sure it'll be a son? It could be a daughter, too."

"Well, let's think of some names," she said.

"Yes, let's do that."

"What's the hurry, my king?" she said, coming closer to him and kissing him slowly on the lips.

At that moment, all stress, all sorrows, all ambitions, all hatred and all responsibilities were forgotten.

48

"My Lord, I come bearing troubling news," the messenger said.

Vritra turned around.

"Speak," he ordered.

"My Lord, Commander Vichitra of the Northern Kalakeyas has been killed. We suspect Devas' involvement. Lakhanjo Daro is under risk."

Vritra held his breath. He controlled his emotions. But his expressions made it clear that it was grave news.

The Devas were already just a week away from the frontiers. If they controlled the City of Lakshman, the war was lost.

Occupying a strategic point in the New Asura Empire, Lakhanjo Daro was an extremely defendable city. Like New Amaravati, the main army could march inland while a small band of only a hundred archers could easily defend the fort.

"Should we direct our army to Lakhan-jo-Daro, my Lord?"

Vritra did not answer. The army could not be changed now of all times. Since conquering more territories, more rebellions had to be crushed. If the Devas conquered it, the Western boundary of the Sindhu would be lost.

"Just tell them to strengthen their defences and stay prepared."

"All right, my Lord."

49

"That's troubling," said Indra.

Dasra had just informed Indra of the Kalakeya occupation of Lakhanjo Daro that he had heard from Vichitra's man before dying.

"So, what do we do?" asked an agitated Varuna.

"We attack. In two months. Till then, they'd have lowered their guard."

"Why two months?" asked Mitra.

"We need more soldiers. Those Vaanars that you saved from the bull can be useful, Brother," said Indra, referring to Mitra's killing of the bull.

"What do you want me to do?"

"You and Varuna Bhaiyya will go to Persia and get them. They shall be provided with homes, and the fittest farmers shall be enrolled in the army."

"When do we leave?" asked Varuna.

"Tomorrow."

"And the Soma?" questioned Mitra.

"That can be delayed. For now, we must drive away the Asuras."

"Ok."

50

The war room was littered with maps, scrolls, war manuals and models of the army units. Miniature models of the infantry, cavalry, chariots and archers were kept on the table.

Hiranyastupa, Tvashtri, Ribhu and his brothers, Mitra, Varuna, Shachi, the twins, Deva nobles, and commanders stood around the large ten-feet by two-feet table.

However, the war room was in total pandemonium.

"No, no, no! You haven't got a basic understanding of war tactics! You're just a noble!" yelled Deva General Aryaman at Lord Bhaga.

Both men were complete opposites of each other.

General Aryaman was a childhood friend and close confidante of Mitra and Varuna. He had taken up the post after his father, a wheezing old man of fifty who had injured his leg in the conflict with the Panis. He was dressed in a light green dhoti and a black leather breastplate. Judging from the sweat and dirt, he had just come from combat practice. Rudraksha beads proudly proclaimed his devotion to Lord Shiva. A lean scimitar hung from his crimson sash. A shawl was hastily thrown over his shoulders for protection from cold. His usually well-maintained hair was now greasy and oily, but it seemed to add to his looks. Three-day-old stubble replaced the usually moustached face that caught the attention of most ladies. A gold chain with a sun pendant hung from his long neck.

Treasurer Bhaga, however, was in stark contrast to the restrained Aryaman. A life of luxury showed itself in the jewellery he wore and the bright pink turban with gold ornaments. Like Aryaman, he, too, wore the sun on his gold chain, though it was a bit overshadowed by the golden sapphire necklace. Opulent though he was, Bhaga was not too unfit or obese. He exercised and practised combat regularly. A gold-sheathed dagger hung from his silk waistband. Due to his opulence, the ministers nicknamed him the 'Original Kuber', referring to the wealthiest man in history, renowned as the God of Wealth and the brother of Raavan, Lord Kuber.

Unlike Aryaman, he was clean-shaven and spent a lot of time in his grooming. Rumours were he spent as much as eight hundred gold coins on beauty products and clothes.

"I'M JUST SUGGESTING A MORE ECONOMIC APPROACH, ARYAMAN! YOU DON'T UNDERSTAND BUSINESS! YOU'RE JUST READY TO DIE IN THE BATTLEFIELD! BUT, I SUGGEST AN OPTION WHERE WE KILL INSTEAD OF DYING IN A GLORIFIC WAY!"

The chaos in the room was getting out of hand.

"QUIET!" yelled Shachi.

The men fell silent.

"Both of you, Shut up!"

The tone of her voice made the men fall silent.

"General Aryaman, what do you suggest?"

"I suggest an aggressive course of action. The fort is made in such a way that it can hold off even the worst attacks from incoming invaders. A human ram from a phalanx will work. We'll need heavy shields. And long spears. That'll soften the enemy lines and grant us victory. A difficult but quick victory."

"Lord Bhaga, what do you propose?" she turned to Bhaga.

Bhaga smiled.

"General Aryaman has forgotten these elevated platforms, My Lady," said Bhaga, pointing to two squares on the perimeter map.

"They can clearly throw hot oil on us from here." continued Bhaga.

"So, here's what I propose. We move from here, and then we will suddenly split up. The phalanx will be rearranged in a needlepoint formation, with Marut chariots riding in the front. Lord Devendra, or whoever he deems fit, will lead the Maruts on an elephant. Our secret weapon, the Indrastra, shall be mounted there. The shrapnel will wound the closely packed Kalakeya formations. Their horses will panic, causing pandemonium, and we shall have won the battle," he beamed brightly.

For the first time in the past quarter of an hour, Aryaman realized the futility of his plan and saw the brilliance in Bhaga's.

"My god, Bhaga! This will work. I ... uh... I apologize for the rudeness earlier," he said, turning beet red.

Bhaga smiled.

"That's a brilliant plan, Lord Bhaga. We must train the soldiers to break formation in time rapidly. Lord Aryaman, you shall be responsible for training the army," said the Devendra.

"As you wish, my king."

"And, the soldiers need new equipment. Also, Nasatya and Dasra require a chariot. Tvashtri, Ribhu, could you possibly hold a workshop for my smiths? They could use your superior knowledge."

"Consider it done, My Lord," said Tvashtri.

"Lord Agni willing, we shall finally control the Sapta-Sindhu," said Hiranyastupa.

"We shall avenge Lord Dadhyanch," added Indra.

Hiranyastupa nodded solemnly.

Tvashtri's day had suddenly become very hectic. He woke half an hour before sunrise, prayed, and then went to the forges. He had to teach the surprisingly inept Deva workers to work with weapons. Ribhu and his brothers were working on the "ladles", while Tvashtri was handling the far more complex and complicated Vajra. He also had the task of replicating more Agneyastras and Indrastras to last for years.

The material he chose to work with after reading Brihaspati's manuscripts was horse bones and steel.

The crystals and electromagnets had been carefully attached with wires to their rightful places in the apparatus. A small electrical source had to be made.

Vashishth had devised an ingenious solution for that. The ceramic cylinders inside the handle contained a solution of particular chemicals and two metal rods connected to the main wire. A small lever would have to be pulled by the wielder of the thunderbolt, which would dip the metal rods in the solution. This would then complete the circuit, and the magnets would start working.

Readjusting the lever would retract the metal rods, and the current would cease.

It was a brilliant weapon. And irreplicable. It was Brihaspati's genius that made it possible to recreate this ancient weapon of the Ancient Gods of Thunder.

51

The fleet was in complete pandemonium. They were two weeks into the middle of the sea. The plan was to sail up the Bolan and then enter the Sindhu when the Bolan joined her. They would then sail out into the open seas and reach the Persian Gulf in nearly three weeks. After which, the Vaanars would be granted refuge in New Amaravati, and the willing ones conscripted in the armies.

However, an unexpected pirate attack was not part of the plan. A fleet of Mleccha dinghies had attacked the mighty Deva ships.

"These fools are outnumbered ten-to-one by us. They have no large ships, no real trained soldiers, no catapults, and they think they can attack us?" said Mitra.

"Should we attack them?" asked the captain.

"No."

"What?"

Mitra grinned. He unclipped the coin pouch from his waistband and threw it at one of the boats. A man picked it up and, looking inside, was shocked to find gold willingly being thrown at him. In disbelief, he gazed at the man who had just thrown him the gold. Mitra waved at the man as the ship was being turned away.

The man's jaw was still on the ground.

"To hell with this wind!" cursed Mitra. The wind had been blowing very slowly, and the hot sun burned Mitra's back. But, more importantly, the boats couldn't move much further, very fast, if the wind was this slow.

"Where are the rowers?" asked Mitra.

"On break," replied Varuna.

Mitra let loose a long line of expletives that vaguely mentioned the rowers' birth processes.

"Oh, come on! Can't you live without swearing? Your son is on deck!" said an exasperated Varuna.

The seventeen-year-old Vashishth barely managed to control his expressions.

Mitra smiled and winked at him.

Varuna sighed.

Sometimes, he was almost glad he had no children.

Vangrida was sitting in his private study. He had received word from Emperor Vritra to improve the defences and prepare the army.

Devas? They're in bloody Amaravati, man!

He read on.

When the hell did they conquer Mehrgarh?!

He then took a decision. The son of Dyaus would not win.

Not as long as I'm here, he mused, his bloodshot eyes narrowing.

52

"It's Lord Mithra!" shouted the three boys as they ran to the village.

Ahura Mithra, the slayer of the bull, the saviour of men, was in the village again. This time, he was accompanied by a man who looked like his twin. Unlike Mitra's dark brown ones, the other man's eyes resembled the waters he had been named after.

"Namaste, Chief Vrishakapi.

"Oh, Lord Mithra! You are radiant as the Sun god! Bless us, oh, mighty warrior!"

Mitra was embarrassed by Vrishakapi's behaviour.

A lean man of nearly forty, Vrishakapi had been one of the younger members of the Vaanar council when the previous Sarpanch had proclaimed Mitra a god. Vrishakapi, too, had lost a friend to the bull. He was indebted to Mitra.

"Rise, Lord Vrishakapi, for you are a friend. Not a servant."

Vrishakapi's moist eyes were a window to his mind that was elated at the prospect of being friends with the finest military leader in Vaanar history after Lord Hanuman.

Quickly changing the topic, Mitra said-

"This is…this is my brother, Varuna, Chief Judicial Officer of the Devas. And this is Vashishth, my son," he said, gazing fondly at the young boy.

Vashishth smiled politely at the old man and folded his hands into a namaste. He then bowed down to touch Vrishakapi's feet. He didn't consider himself worthy enough to get his feet touched by the Saviour's feet. Equally though, he didn't want to be rude.

He blessed the boy with a long life.

"Let's come into the fort, Lord," invited Vrishakapi.

Mitra, Varuna and the entourage obliged and marched into the fortress.

"Hey, men! Do you remember that hill?" said Mitra, pointing to the hill where they had camped before when searching for the Vajra.

"How could we forget? That was the best time of my life. Away from my wife, of course."

The men laughed uproariously. Varuna shook his head and followed Mitra into the fortress.

Vrishakapi, eager to please Mitra, showed the entire fort.

"My Lord, these walls were built five centuries ago. They are special because they have been made from a single piece of rock carved into three-and-a-half walls. The fourth wall is a later addition. Till a few centuries back, there were no walls there. Only acacia fences."

"I see," responded Mitra.

"Over here, these are the magnificent gardens. We call it Madhuvan. All sorts of fresh flowers, fruits and honey can be found here," said Vrishakapi.

"Wait! This area is a desert. Where are you getting the water from?" asked an incredulous Varuna.

"Oh, we harvest the rains. We have deep wells in the middle of the city. There is a small seasonal stream as well. It flows in spring, and we gather as much water as possible."

Varuna smiled. Necessity truly was the mother of invention.

"My Lords, if you are tired, we can visit the guest house, and you may rest. I can show you the city tomorrow."

"That would be a wonderful idea, Chief Vrishakapi."

"Also, feel free to eat the fruit. The garden is yours. I've heard that the apples are exceptionally juicy and delicious this time of the year."

"That would be wonderful," Mitra said politely.

"We can meet tomorrow to discuss the matter that bothers you," said Vrishakapi.

"Man, this pudding is awesome! What is this?" asked Mitra, digging out almonds from the rice and milk dish in his bowl.

"Oh, this? This is a staple of our people. It is known as Tasmai. It is made from sweetened milk, cardamoms, saffron, almonds and rice," said Vrishakapi.

"You people are lucky. We Devas don't have these kinds of good meals."

"You are being too kind, My Lord."

Saying so, Vrishakapi exited the dining hall of the guest house, leaving Mitra to himself.

"Did Lord Mitra send a letter darling?" enquired Shachi.

"No, Love," replied the stressed-out Indra.

"No need to fret. I'm sure everything is all right," she reassured him.

"Forget about that. Tell me, how is the future king of the Devas doing?"

"Or Queen."

"Of course, King or Queen."

"Or maybe both," she smiled knowingly.

"Both? Are…are we having twins?!" he asked, tears of happiness glistening in his eyes.

She smiled.

The twins of Indra, the God of Thunder.

53

Preparations for the war had started full swing. Sacrifices to the great War Gods, Lord Mangal; Lord Agni; Lord Skand; the warrior form of Lord Shiva; the first Devendra, Lord Indra; Lord Narasimha; Goddess Durga; Lord Hanuman and the various family gods of soldiers had begun.

A grand yagna that would last for weeks had also been organized. The priests would be given massive amounts of riches as alms, including hundreds of cows, horses, clothes, and gold. The kitchen had been working in full swing to prepare food for the Brahmins.

Despite her weakness, Shachi was overseeing the work in the kitchens.

"No! The priests specifically asked for offerings without salt!"

Making food for the Brahmins, the soldiers and the offering proved challenging. As per the Vedic rites, Lord Surya, the Sun God, could not be offered food with salt.

"So, should I just throw it away?" the maid asked timidly.

"Are you crazy? The soldiers and the priests will consume it, for the gods' sake!"

The maid hurried away, lowering her head and averting her eyes.

"Hurry up! It's nearly sunrise!" she shouted.

The cooks had to begin making food three hours before sunrise. There was hardly any time for rest. Yet, Shachi managed it all efficiently without a chair. And with five-month-old twins growing rapidly inside her belly.

"Your Highness, it's been one month. There has been no attack on Lakhanjo Daro yet," said the spy.

Vritra had sent multiple letters to Vangrida to stay prepared and train the army. No reply had come from him, too. Vritra knew how lazy the man was.

"Any news from Vangrida?"

"None so far, Your Highness."

"Did he reply to the scroll that I sent?"

"He just sent a messenger who said not to worry."

Vritra fell into contemplation. The Dream of the Kalakeya empire must be realized.

"The other frontier towns?"

"Safe as of now."

"Any revolts?"

"None since the last one, six months back."

Vritra sighed.

"There's another thing, Your Highness."

"What?"

"Chief Vangrida has been found consorting with the Nivatakavachas. We think he plans to rebel."

"That bastard!"

The Nivatakavachas were the other major Asura clan. The Kalakeyas, who were united under Vritra, were the major ones. The Nivatakavachas were brutal enemies of the Kalakeyas.

Before the Kurukshetra war, the Kalakeya-Nivatakavacha alliance was one of the most fearsome militaries of ancient times. So fierce even the Devendras required Divyastras to defeat them. Naval battles with the world's finest navigators proved disastrous for the Devas.

However, the Devendra's son, Lord Arjun, was an exceptional warrior. He defeated the armies single-handedly and resent them to Pataal. The Nivatakavachas and the Kalakeyas blamed each other. What was a drunken brawl turned into an armed conflict. Leaders were assassinated, Generals bribed, kidnappings became commonplace incidents and children of noble families were targeted.

The conflict came to an end with the Kalakeya-Daitya migration to the Sapta-Sindhu.

"How do you know?" enquired Vritra agitatedly.

"Important Nivatakavacha ministers have been discovered in Lakhanjo Daro. Also, spy reports say that a few letters have been discovered from the Nivatakavacha King."

"Send a message. Ask for eight hundred soldiers. I shall sign it personally. That bastard shall rot and burn there. Make sure the Devas get news of it."

"Right away, my Lord."

"That traitor should not get suspicious."

Saying so, Vritra clutched the hundred-and-eight beaded rosary on his table and began chanting the name of Lord Hari.

Hari.

Hari.

Hari.

Hari.

Vangrida was sweating profusely.

"Chief Suviryavan, I apologize, but if the Chief Kalakeya, Lord Vritra, finds out about the betrayal-"

"He'll die before that," replied the man calmly.

'Nivatakavacha' literally meant 'armour-bodied'. This referred to the fact that their warriors continued to fight even after multiple wounds.

A muscular man of nearly thirty, the Chief of the Nivatakavachas was extremely fit and strong. An expert in mace warfare, Suviryavan knew how to attack with lances, swords, bows, daggers, and flails.

Reaching the height of seven feet, Suviryavan was the tallest man Vangrida had ever seen. Handlebar moustaches sat proudly on his upper lips. A silver crown concealed his prematurely receding hairline. However, even without the crown, his intimidating presence outshone his hairline. He was dressed in a red dhoti and black angavastra.

"My apologies, but don't you think it would be wise if we were to openly rebel?"

Suviryavan gave him a hard stare. Vangrida fell silent.

"I need to go back to Pataal today. You have three weeks. Make a decision. If you refuse, you die."

Saying so, Suviryavan got up and wiped his face with his angavastra. Then he turned his back and went out of the room.

Vangrida stared at the retreating back of the Nivatakavacha ruler.

54

The Yagna continued with the usual prayers to Lord Agni and his wife, Lady Swaha, followed by salutations to the primordial Devendra, Lord Indra and finally, the pause. During the break, the Brahmins consumed their meals, and Indra sneaked off to meet Shachi in the kitchens.

"Stop it," she hissed. "Get the hell out of here!"

Indra pouted in mock anger and pretended to be sad like a spoilt child.

Shachi smiled and pushed him outside.

"Can I at least get a kiss?"

She smiled and pecked him on the cheek.

He smiled and ran off. On the way, Tvashtri bumped into his arm and nearly dropped the Vajra on the ground.

"Careful!" exclaimed Indra.

"Good morning to you, Great King," beamed Tvashtri cheerfully.

"I'm sorry, Tvashtri," apologized Indra.

"At least the thunderbolt is safe," said Tvashtri.

"I hope you didn't get hurt," said Indra.

Tvashtri waved his hand dismissively.

"How are the forges?" enquired Indra.

Tvashtri's expression made it clear that it was tedious work. The incompetent, mostly Gandharva and Yakshadominated Deva workforce was not used to following orders. Ribhu and Vaja were the frequent subjects of the common pranks played by the tricksters.

"It's... It's difficult... sometimes," said a hesitating Tvashtri.

Indra smiled.

"Hey, can I ask you something?"

"Anything, My Lord," said Tvashtri.

"Would you like to join the war?"

Tvashtri gulped. Had the man gotten suspicious? Did he want to keep him so as to restrict his freedom? Flattery didn't always work. And Tvashtri knew that.

"I...I don't think it would be possible for me. You're a king, and I..."

"The true mark of a king is treating a craftsman and the crown prince the same."

"I... but, no! That's not the reason. I... I have to go on a pilgrimage."

"What? When?"

"Uh... it's just a week before the war."

"All right. Just come to the war room tonight. We can discuss some strategy tonight before you go."

"It would be my honour," said a moist-eyed Tvashtri.

All that mattered now was the mission.

The rider seemed uneasy. He kept turning back to look at some invisible or possibly non-existent threat. His face was carefully concealed with a white turban and black mask. A knee-length khaki tunic, brown leather boots and sandy dhoti camouflaged him in the desert sand. He was no more than five feet and six inches in height.

The camel on which he was riding seemed highly bored. With the usual constipated smile typical of its species, the camel was chewing its semi–digested last meal in a disgusting daily ritual. Unruly strands of white acidic enzymes escaped out of its mouth. Its long feet were treading softly on the sand.

The rider's entire body moved gracefully with the rhythmic rise and fall of the beast's buttocks. He suddenly pulled the reins, and the camel stopped. The man shoved his heel lightly into the beast's abdomen as it bent its front knees and began to sit down. This was followed by the movement of the rear legs, and the camel was completely on the ground, giving the rider the experience of seasickness on dry land in the middle of a desert.

The rider took a moment to clear his head and drank water from his hip flask. The camel made a familiar grunting noise. The man pulled the reins, and the camel stood up, repeating the above process in reverse and in the time it took for you to read from the beginning of this page to here. The camel widened his rear legs and shot a continuous stream of golden, syrupy piss from its shrunken organ .

The man removed his mask and allowed his face to cool. He was a short, bald man of nearly sixty. A frail beard covered his chin, and his moustache reached his lower jaw. Hair emerged from his ears, and his right temple had a burn mark. His distinguishing features made people recognize him instantly and remember his face— a bad thing in a secret mission.

He quickly pulled out a dagger and a flint from his pouch. While praying to Lord Agni, he rubbed the two and started a fire. He then pulled out some food wrapped in a paper parcel from the pouch and began to heat it in a clay vessel.

Once it was hot, he emptied it into a plate and picked up the hip flask. He gently took some water in his hand and sprinkled it around his plate. Then he picked up a morsel and placed it aside as an offering to the gods. Before eating the first bite, he chanted the Bhojanam Mantra prayer.

Annapate annasyano dehyanamīvasya śuṣmiṇaḥ pra pradātāraṃ tāriṣa

ūrjanno dhehi dvipade catuṣpade

Svādo pīto madho pīto vayaṃ tvā vavṛmahe asmākamavītā bhava

Moghamannam vindate apracetāḥ satyaṃ bravīmi vadha itsatasya

nāryamaṇaṃ puṣyati no sakhāyaṃ kevalāgho bhavati kevalādī oṃ śāntiḥ

[May food be beneficial for the body.
May everyone be blessed with food.
O! Giver of food, may you provide us with energy.

The foolish man wins food with fruitless labour.
That food I speak the
truth shall be his ruin. Who feeds no man, no friend shall
love him. All guilt is he who eats alone.
Let there be peace.]

55

Indra clutched Mitra in a hug with his arms spread wide open. The twins, Nasatya and Dasra rushed out of the palace to greet Varuna. They bent down to touch his feet.

"May you live long," blessed Varuna.

"Now, where are the Vaanars?" enquired Indra.

"Lord Indra, I would like you to meet Chief Vrishakapi, the Overlord of the Persian Vaanars," said Mitra.

"Lord Devendra, we have heard stories of your mighty conquests, how your clever strategies defeated the Pani tribes. We are honoured to have been here with the Devas."

"The pleasure's all ours, Chief Vrishakapi."

"I heard that you required our assistance in your battle. We wish to reclaim our ancient lands in the South of the Sapta-Sindhu. The Kalakeya supremacy shall not prevail! Har Har Mahadev!" said the Vaanar, repeating the ancient war cry of the devotees of Lord Shiva.

"HAR HAR MAHADEV!" repeated the Vaanars.

Indra smiled at the confidence and courage of the legendary warriors.

"You may be feeling a bit seasick after your sojourn. I request you all to stay in the guest house. The Angiras shall be here to keep you company."

"The Angiras?" asked Vrishakapi, his eyes widening in a pleasant surprise.

"Yes, in fact, we have their leader here with us! Lord Hiranyastupa!" called Indra.

"Namaste, oh Chief of the Vaanars," said Hiranyastupa politely.

"Oh, my Lord! It's an honour to meet a man of your stature here!" said Vrishakapi.

"Thank you! And I hope that wasn't a pun!" said Hiranyastupa, referring to his short stature. He barely reached the five-feet-and eleven-inches-tall Vrishakapi's shoulder.

The men laughed loudly, and Indra slapped Vrishakapi playfully on the shoulder.

Like most Vaanars, Vrishakapi was huge. Nearly reaching six feet. He had club-like biceps. Like most Vaanars, he shaved his moustaches and kept just a full beard—disfigured jaws, common amongst Vaanars and an extra thumb added to the air of awkwardness around him. His muscular frame was adorned by a knee-length red dhoti with a green sash and a sky-blue angavastra. Leather sandals and a single gold and emerald necklace completed the warrior look.

"Well, if the jokes are finished, I would like to show you to your room, Vrishakapi ji," said Indra.

"Of course, My Lord. But don't bother. We shall go by ourselves. You just tell us where the room is."

"No, no, it's fine!" said Indra.

"No, we don't want to trouble you on our first day here!"

Indra gave in with a sigh. Devotion could be difficult at times to deal with.

"By the gods! What the hell is that monkey group doing?!" said a surprised guard to another.

It had been a week since the Vaanars' arrival. And they had already begun brewing trouble. The pride of Mehrgarh, adjacent to the guest house, the Vatika garden palace, was being torn apart by some young Vaanars. Unlike in the Madhuvan gardens, the fruits and honey here were neither free nor open to the public. Instead of the Vatika palace, the smaller and less beautiful park was open to the guests.

"Stop those monkeys!" ordered the Deva security chief, Pushan.

A five-feet ten-inches tall man, Pushan had once been a Marut. However, he had been positioned inside the city to command the unorganised Deva police. A lifetime of strict military discipline and an incredible memory of roads and ways did not restrict him from making jokes about everything in sight.

He had to control himself frequently to not crack jokes at inappropriate moments, such as at a funeral or an unhappy marriage.

He usually dressed in a white angavastra and blue dhoti.

His good nature and handsome looks made him popular amongst the Deva city defence force.

"WAIT!" shouted Indra as he ran to the men.

"Lord Indra," said the soldiers, saluting in the Deva fashion.

"They're our guests! We can't just…"

"Fall back," ordered Pushan as the men obeyed.

"Chief Vrishakapi is also there with them," said Indra.

"We are sorry, my Lord," apologised Pushan.

"Come on, man!" said Indra.

Pushan smiled his familiar, disarming grin.

The Vaanars were still busy and did not notice the cops.

They are monkeys, mused Pushan.

The lone rider was still three days away from the city of Lakhanjo Daro. One of the biggest sprawling cities in the Sapta-Sindhu, its condition had deteriorated rapidly under the Asura rule. Though unlike other Sapta-Sindhu cities, the Asuras were still a minority here.

The city had been founded by Lord Ram's sons, Lord Lava and Lord Kush. It had been named in honour of their uncle, Lord Lakshman and originally called Lakshmandurg, Lakshman's fort. The Gandharva rendition of the name stuck since the Asuras renounced all things Deva, including the language Sanskrit.

A debt should be paid off till the last cowrie and the enemy destroyed till the last man.

56

"That monkey destroyed my rose plants! The ones which you gave me!" said an infuriated Shachi.

"Oh, hey! Relax!" said Indra.

It was midnight. The yagna was completed yesterday, so Shachi did not have to get too troubled now. Or at least, she thought it meant that.

"Relax? That bastard destroyed my rose bushes, and you're telling me to relax? Tell that hyperactive friend of yours to relax, Indra!"

Indra laughed at her choice of words. Military life had gifted her a violent sense of humour.

"Come on! It's not like it's the end of the world."

She remained cross and he kissed her on the cheek. She still didn't say anything.

"All right, I need to sleep," announced Indra before opening the blanket at his feet.

The last thing he saw before dozing off was the swollen belly of Shachi, the current home of his progeny.

57

"What?" asked Vangrida.

Vritra's spy had just come from Mehrgarh. The Devas were assembling as they spoke. The spy showed him the battle formations. The chariots and infantry were in particular positions.

This would mean that they knew the exact layout of the fort!

"I'll be damned!" exclaimed Vangrida. It was evident from the positions of the cavalry that the western wall would be the main centre of the attack. However, an unusual detail was that the attack would be concentrated solely on the western wall, in a battering ram formation meant to break open the gates.

"When will they reach?" asked Vangrida.

The masked man held up five fingers to show five days.

"Turvasu!" shouted Vangrida.

A bald servant of twenty-two with a small braid at the back of his head entered the room. He was dressed in a white dhoti and yellow angavastra, folded into a towel-like shape and hanging loosely from his left shoulder to the small of his back. A janeu ran from his left shoulder to the right side of the waist.

"Yes, my Lord," he answered meekly.

"Get me the general from the barracks and a small snack platter, too," he ordered.

The servant hurried off. He had learnt not to question his master's whims. The countless lash marks on his back taught him that.

The servant returned a quarter of an hour later with the general and a plate loaded with wine, chalices, bread and chutney. He quietly placed it on the table and rushed out on the tips of his toes, afraid that his master would explode like a bomb.

"You must be hungry," said Vangrida.

Unmindful of his growling stomach, the spy did not reach out for the proffered food; he couldn't risk showing his face in the middle of his mission.

"If you say so," shrugged Vangrida, stuffing bread into his mouth as he poured himself a big cup of wine.

"Oh, my bad!" said Vangrida with his mouth full, slapping his right hand on the forehead.

"This is—" his sentence was cut short by a burp.

"Pardon me, this is General Shambara," he said.

Shambara was a common Kalakeya name, which referred to a species of deer. Though it was a Sanskrit name, many great Asura leaders of the past were named Shambara. Hence, it remained popular even after the abolition of Sanskrit.

General Shambara was sixty. His physical appearance could, however, be deceiving. A clever military mind, accompanied by a ruthless ambition to spread the Kalakeya Supremacy around the globe, made a bad combination. If a riot went out of hand, he would be called. And that was when the revolters, mostly non-Asuras, lost. They lost before the war began.

Dressed in a black dhoti and brown shawl, the intimidating General Shambara had a toothbrush moustache. His salt-and-pepper beard looked more like stubble. His grey eyes were cold like the snowy mountains of the Himalayas.

The masked man bowed his head to the General, who gave a curt nod in acknowledgement.

"General, would you please look here?" said Vangrida.

The General stared at the rough map and the chess figures representing the Deva armies.

"Damn, that seems serious!" said the General.

"So what strategy should be adopted?"

"Please leave," the General said to the spy. Though the tone was polite, it was an order, not a request.

"Oh, relax! He's Lord Vritra's man," said Vangrida.

"Show us your face," ordered Shambara.

"I can't do that. I have to stay hidden. Lord Vritra has permitted me to do so," said the man, showing an official scroll bearing the seal of the Firstborn of The Dragons himself.

"All right. Seems fair enough," shrugged Shambara.

Shambara held Vritra in deep regard. He managed to do what no Asura leader had done for centuries. The divided Kalakeya tribes had been finally unified. The Firstborn of The Dragons controlled nearly the entire Sapta-Sindhu. And expansion into the rest of Aryavarta? Piece of cake.

"So, here's our strategy," said Shambara. "We station all our troops on the Western wall. The Eastern has no risk, the Northern is too thick, and the Southern would be easily defendable."

The man under the mask smiled.

58

"Set out!" shouted Aryaman.

The Deva armies would march out for the Fort of Lakshman today. Nearly twenty thousand men of tremendous courage stood on the gates of Mehrgarh. Indra climbed up the stairs of the bastion to give a speech.

"Devas! Gandharvas! Rakshasas! Yakshas! Vaanars!" he addressed the crowd.

Roars from the Vaanars and Rakshasas met his enthusiasm. Historical enemies, circumstances and fate united them after Lord Sugreev and Lord Vibhishana's treaty after the Battle in Lanka that solved the territory dispute.

"Lord Ram said that Mother and Motherland are superior to paradise! Our motherland is threatened! What kind of warriors would we be if we can't even defend our motherland? For too long have the Daityas ravaged the country. It was the Kurukshetra War which weakened us. The War for Dharma, where all laws were broken. It was a result of this Adharma that the Asuras took over. We have committed enough penance to compensate—one millennium. Now, our Dharma is being tested again. It would be Adharma to leave our motherland undefended. Do we commit the same mistakes again?"

"NO!" thundered the crowd.

"Are we on the side of Dharma or Adharma?"

"DHARMA!"

"We are Devas! WE ARE GODS!"

"YATO DHARMASTATO JAYAH!" thundered the energised crowd.

Yato Dharmastato jayah. An ancient chant which meant where there is Dharma, there is victory.

"SATYAMEVA JAYATE!" shouted Mitra for good measure.

"SATYAMEVA JAYATE!" shouted the crowd.

Satyameva Jayate.

Truth always conquers.

"Wake up," said an exasperated Ambika.

Mohenjo-Daro was buzzing with gossip. Bactrian forces were closing in around Lakhanjo Daro.

Just think, thought Ambika. *Deva forces are getting closer day by day, and this man is sleeping like a baby!*

Ambika was the wife of the present Rudra, Pashupati. They had been married some time back, even before he became Rudra.

"Pashupati," she said again.

"Mphhh..." he grunted.

"Wake up! Deva forces are nearing," she said urgently.

He instantly arose.

"What?"

"Yes," she said. He smiled.

The Devas were always on the side of Dharma. That was why every avatar of Lord Vishnu was on the Devas' side.

The Rudra's task was to enforce the rule of law on the earth by destroying the decadent civilisation. That was why many dangerous Astras were under the Bhutaganas' control.

"We need to ally with them," said Pashupati.

Ambika nodded, tears in her eyes. The Devas were the ancient tribe revered as the gods that Ambika worshipped.

"We need to reach their current location. Secretly," he added.

"I'll get two horses ready," she said. He nodded.

The camel rider was out in the dunes when he saw it. The cloud of dust. And from among the dust emerged golden breastplates and helmets. The weak rays of the evening sun reflected off the armour but cloaked the faces. But the rider recognised them.

Maruts!

He quickly dismounted and left the camel where it was. Then he ran to the nearest tallest dune. Climbing up slowly, he lay face-down in the sand and concealed himself. His sandy clothes cloaked him well.

Thank the gods I shaved!

A loud conch shell war trumpet was heard.

General Aryaman and Commander Pushan rode out to the front as the Maruts stopped.

"We make camp here," said Pushan.

The Deva armies were commanded by eight to twelve commanders, known as *Adityas*. These were temporary wartime positions and could change. Nasatya's father, Savitar, was also one.

The current Adityas were Indra, Mitra, Varuna, Aryaman, Pushan, Bhaga, Anshuman and Martand.

Anshuman was Aryaman's twin brother. They were alike in physique but as apart as pork and peas in personality. While Anshuman preferred spear combat, Aryaman preferred swords. While Anshuman enjoyed philosophy, Aryaman despised it completely and preferred straight answers.

Martand was the new commander of the Maruts. After Shachi's pregnancy, a trained leader to command the Maruts was required. At the time of Shachi's retirement, Martand was a lieutenant General, one of the highest posts in the Deva military. Dressed nearly always in a knee-length tunic and war boots, Martand had a long moustache that he maintained lovingly.

When he was born, he was actually stillborn until the wet nurse suckled him. His name reflected that. *Martand, the dead egg.*

"Lord Devendra, it is nearly sunset. Should we go for some late-night hunting?" asked Dasra longingly.

Indra smiled. It was on.

59

Nasatya, Dasra and Indra were out hunting. It was way after midnight. Yet, an unsuccessful hunt before a war was a bad omen.

When they were losing hope, movement sounds were heard from the cluster of bushes. It was a boar!

"Quick, shoot!" ordered Indra.

Before the boar could even blink, an arrow from Nasatya and another from Dasra lodged into its neck; it struggled in agony as it rolled in the dust.

Indra drew out a sword and cleanly sliced off its head in one swift stroke.

"Phew! At least it's not unsuccessful," said Nasatya.

"Thank Lord Agni," whispered Dasra.

"Hey, wait!" said Indra as he noticed something on the slopes of the hill as he went closer.

The shrub seemed oddly familiar. He had seen its drawing somewhere.

He looked at it a bit more. Then he remembered.

Brihaspati's manuscripts. Dhatura!

"Hey, help me load it into my saddlebag. It can be used in the Somaras," he added, knowing that teenagers did nothing without knowing the reason.

As expected, the boys set out to work hearing about the Drink of The Gods, the Elixir of Immortality.

"By the gods! That's curious," exclaimed Hiranyastupa.

"What's so curious?" asked Indra.

"It's just that Dhatura, here, in these parts, is very rare. I was thinking of sending some men to the far north to search for it."

"So, how much Soma can be made with this amount."

"Well, the Dhatura and Soma extract ratio with milk should be 1:2 in that order. But to make it less intoxicating, we need a few more ingredients."

"Like what?"

"Like mead. Spiced mead. Mead with added cinnamon, green cardamom and ginger."

"And can we make it now? Today?"

Hiranyastupa smiled. He had come prepared for it.

He pulled out a clay vial from his satchel. It emitted a bitter smell that was oddly addictive.

"This is fermented Soma extract," explained Brihaspati.

"Now, all it needs is some milk and water. Can you get me some? Cow milk works the best."

Indra nodded and rushed out. A few minutes later, he emerged with a cup of milk and a glass of water.

Hiranyastupa carefully added both substances in equal amounts.

Bubbles began to escape as the milk dissolved into the extract.

"Pass the Dhatura shrubs, please."

Indra obliged.

He beat the shrub into powder and dissolved it in the remaining water. The crushed seeds did not dissolve. Instead, they floated on the top.

"Now we just stir it up a bit and leave it on the fire to boil."

Indra was carefully observing the process.

"I need a little honey and clarified butter," announced Hiranyastupa.

"Why the honey and butter?"

"Well, they act as a substitute for the mead. Also, Brahmins don't drink."

Indra nodded and rushed off to get the clarified butter and honey.

Hiranyastupa waited for Indra as he set the cup of Dhatura tea to boil. The infusion would have to simmer till it changed colour to a dark caramel shade. The infusion took its time to boil as the fire was small. But after it did boil, Hiranyastupa placed a cloth around the rim and strained it using a piece of muslin fabric from an old angavastra.

By this time, Indra had returned with two pots, one with honey and another with *ghrita.* Under his arm was tucked a manuscript of Brihaspati.

"Thank you so much, Great Lord. Most nobles wouldn't even do such a small task."

Indra, embarrassed at being called Great, instead changed the topic.

"So..."

"Nearly there. Patience, my king. The fruits of patience are always juicy," he smiled.

The boiled tea was kept in a metallic vessel so it wouldn't cool. And the Soma with milk was still bubbling.

"Impure air is leaving the vessel," he explained.

Hiranyastupa pulled out a pack of spices he always carried while travelling and crushed one cinnamon, two green cardamoms, one clove, one black pepper and dried ginger.

"It improves the taste."

Hiranyastupa waited for the last bubbles to disappear before adding the spice mix to the ghrita and honey mixture. The Dhatura tea was still hot. Mixing the three elements into two kulhads, Hiranyastupa scooped some out of his and Indra's before offering it to the flames. He then chanted specific Mantras to offer the Soma to Lord Agni and the Devendras of the past.

"This yagna sends the fumes of the Soma into your lungs and clears your airways."

After half an hour, when the ceremony was complete, Hiranyastupa offered one cup to Indra and took the other for himself.

"To the gods," he whispered, moist-eyed.

"To the gods," repeated Indra.

60

"By the gods, my…my head hurts," said Indra after waking up.

Tiredness led him to sleep in Hiranyastupa's hut, where he had just woken up.

"It's working," nodded Hiranyastupa with a smile.

"Damn! My sinuses! They're burning," he added.

"It happens to everyone when they take the Somaras for the first time," explained the wizened Brahmin.

"Ugh, my guts just want to leap out! .I just feel so… nauseous. So…constipated…"

"You need to stop, my friend," said Hiranyastupa.

"Here, take this. It'll calm you down."

Indra sniffed it. It seemed to be a tea of cannabis and wine.

Sniff.

With just a hint of poppy.

Hiranyastupa smiled. "Go on. It won't bite you," he softly encouraged.

Indra drained the goblet right to its dregs in one sip and fell back on the cot, groaning and clutching his stomach.

"Oh, come on! Are you sure *you* defeated the Panis?" he mocked.

Indra tried to say something, but only a large burp came out. Hiranyastupa chuckled.

Indra tried to retort, but the cannabis and opium were spreading their munificence. He was getting lulled to sleep. And…

Total blackout.

"Brother! Brother!" Mitra said urgently.

Indra opened his eyes. His headache and stomach bouts were gone. And he felt…

New. That was the word. He felt stronger, physically and mentally. He felt faster. He could recollect things faster than usual.

The Somaras!

"Where is Hiranyastupa ji?" he enquired.

"That bastard tried to poison you! Dhatura and opium were found in your mouth. I was passing by the hut and heard a clang. I entered and saw the traitor trying to pick up a knife!" said a livid Mitra.

"It's not what you think!" said an astonished Indra, getting up.

"Oh, come on!" protested Mitra.

Indra grabbed his angavastra hanging from a chair and rushed out of the chamber while straightening it.

Mitra raised his hands in exasperation and followed him to the temporary prison tent set up just for the leader of the Angiras.

The Marut guards removed their lances that were blocking the entrance of the King of The Devas. Indra acknowledged them with a slight nod of his proud head. He entered the tent to find a shackled Hiranyastupa reading a manuscript.

"Lord Devendra," he tried to stand up, but the ropes tying him did not allow him to stand up.

"With all due respect, forgive me for not giving you the respect you deserve. Bad knees," he smiled.

"Cut the chains," he ordered.

"What? No! He poisoned you!" protested Mitra.

"Shall I tell him?" Indra asked Hiranyastupa.

Hiranyastupa nodded.

"That wasn't poison. It was the Somaras."

Mitra's eyes opened wide.

"But, it's supposed to strengthen you! Not weaken you!" argued Mitra.

Indra punched the wooden desk next to Hiranyastupa, where the manuscript had just been. He kicked it hard. Instead of falling and hurting Indra's leg, the table splintered, cracked, fell in fragments, and then hurt Indra's foot.

"DAMN!" he cursed.

"The little toe hurts the most," winced Mitra.

Indra tried to punch him on the shoulder, but Mitra swerved, and Indra lost his balance and fell to the floor.

Mitra laughed uproariously. Indra pulled his dhoti, and it nearly got loose.

All the men in the room laughed softly.

The greatest of blessings and the greatest of follies was joy during times of war.

61

"Stop!" ordered Bhairav.

Pashupati had called the previous Rudra and his two-hundred yogi warriors to aid in an attack on Vangrida's fort. The Deva rule must be reinstated in the Sapta-Sindhu.

The country needed a new system. As Bhairav put it, systems of government were like loincloths. They must be changed regularly.

That was the reason why the Vedas were transmitted orally. They had to change with the times.

"Lord Bhairav, when will we reach the rendezvous point?" enquired Markandeya.

"If you are bored, I won't stop you. Go find a girl," he smiled.

"There is no one like you, Oh Great Destroyer of Death," said Markandeya.

Bhairav sighed. He hated it when Markandeya slipped into one of those devotional moods of his.

He's going to die single.

62

"My Lord, we should make camps in these caves. Not only are they the closest hidden spot to Lakhanjo Daro, but the men are too tired to carry on," said Martand.

Indra nodded his consent. Martand rushed off to convey the orders.

Indra sighed audibly. This campaign lasted longer than expected; he longed to sleep in Shachi's soft embrace.

"Penny for your thoughts?" asked Mitra, interrupting his reverie.

"Oh, hello. Uh, nothing. Just thinking about home."

Mitra smiled. Nothing was better than the loving embrace of your wife. He, too, was thinking about his wife, Urvashi. Comparable in beauty to the Apsaras, Urvashi meant 'she who controlled the hearts of others'.

Born in a rich noble family in Eastern Amaravati, she had always admired warriors. Learning warfare in Gurukul was the first time the eighteen-year-old had laid eyes on Mitra. Two years younger than her, he had already begun training for war.

When the guru had pitted them against one another, it was the first time she had made physical contact with him. One thing led to another, and they married in Gandharva fashion two years later.

The simple wedding was followed by a grand ceremony three weeks later.

Just the following year, Urvashi was pregnant with Vashishth. Varuna, the bookish twin, had begun researching ancient manuscripts in the library. He was always accompanied by fresh bits of ancient knowledge.

In honour of his brother, Mitra had formally named his son Vashishth Maitravaruni; the son of Mitra and Varuna.

"Can't wait to get it over with."

Mitra nodded.

"It's just till tomorrow," he said.

Indra nodded as they stared at the marvellous sunset. The dusk brought with her shades of pink, purple and orange before they would be swallowed by the primaeval darkness, interrupted here and there by the stars. The calm and gentle moon was not a privilege afforded by the earth this new moon night.

"Do you think they are prepared for us?" asked Indra.

"Even if they are, man, they are in for a surprise! Your mount?" he enquired.

Indra would go for a peace treaty on the back of an elephant. His mount: Airavata.

Named after the legendary vehicle of Lord Indra I, Airavata was one of the last few white elephants on the planet. Technically light pink, moonlight made him look light greyish white. An albino, he couldn't see well and was nearly blind. He was a gift to Dyaus during his final years.

Indra had practically stayed by Airavata's side every day through his youth. The elephant treated him like his own brother.

"Ready," answered Indra.

"What clothes are you going to wear?" asked Mitra.

"All white and a gold crown."

"And who's going to accompany you?"

"Martand, Pushan, Aryaman, Anshuman, Varuna, you and Bhaga."

"Hey, where's that Tvashtri guy?"

"Still on pilgrimage."

"And if they don't agree?"

"Call the Adityas. We discuss strategy now."

Little did the two men know they were being spied upon by the little man in the veiled turban who was peeping through a crack in the cave ceiling.

Indra was standing in the private temporary tent consecrated as his war temple. It was built in typical Deva fashion, with a keyhole-shaped design and even a dome made of cloth and bamboo. He had dressed well for the ceremony, with a snow-white dhoti and white silk angavastra with gold border.

The dome's centre was placed directly over the idols, the Holy Trinity, the Trimurti, and the triple gods.

The centre was occupied by a footlong statue of Lord Vishnu standing on two legs. Unlike other gods, Lord Vishnu's idol was influenced by the looks of the previous avatar. Having four arms and a serene smile on his face, his hands held the mighty Sudarshan Chakra, Krishna's famed disc of destruction and a conch, symbol of regeneration and purity. The other two hands were held up in blessing. He was dressed in yellow clothes and wore a crown.

On his right side was the Creative Energy of the Universe, Lord Hiranyagarbha, the first Brahma. He had four heads and four hands, one holding a *kamandalu.*

And on the left was Lord Sadashiv, the first representative of Shiva—the first Rudra. Seated in a yogic posture, hands on his knees and eyes half-closed in a meditative trance, the symbols on his body had their own story to tell.

Though, at first glance, they seemed religious, observation revealed otherwise. Matted locks that captured the Ganga in them symbolised a calm mind that could tame nature.

A crescent moon on his head showed that Lord Shiva accepted everyone regardless of their blemishes, like the moon, which had spots on it.

The serpent around his neck symbolised kundalini, the dormant yogic power residing in everyone.

The trident symbolised the three states of the Universe: Sattva, or bliss; Rajas, or action; and Tamas, or lethargy. Mastery over the three made one a seer who reached the fourth state, Tureeya or Nirvana. Salvation.

Indra bowed to the three idols and went to Lord Sadashiv's murti. He hoped for a war, not peace. He wanted to be remembered as a Warrior. So, he bowed his head to the Energy of Destruction of the Universe.

"*Om tryambakam yyajamahe, sugandhim pushhti-vardhanam.*

Urvarukamiva bandhanaan mrityormukshiya maaamritaat," he prayed.

The Universe sacrifices to the three-eyed one who leads us from the bad to the good smell, which increases our riches.

Like the cucumber being separated from its stalk, may we be separated from death, life and agelessness.

After praying, he tried to meditate but just couldn't concentrate.

"Oh, screw it!" he cursed, unmindful of the presence of the gods, and rushed out.

63

"My Lord, the Devas are here for the peace conference," announced the nervous Turvasu.

Vangrida nearly dropped the wine goblet he was drinking from.

"I'll be there," he said weakly.

The Nivatakavachas were still not here, and the Deva armies stood outside the fort. The Firstborn had mysteriously demanded eight hundred soldiers.

"I'm coming," he said feebly. One could almost pity him if it were not for his atrocities.

Turvasu rushed out, refusing to make any comments. Suddenly, he felt rough hands grabbing his neck. A sweet-smelling, sedative-soaked rag was shoved on his mouth and nose. He fell unconscious within seconds.

Turvasu slowly opened his eyes. A man was obstructing the light. He couldn't see his face, but he recognised the build.

Pipru!

Pipru was one of the personal servants of Vangrida. However, the role of chief of staff had not been offered to him. It had instead gone to Turvasu.

"Pipru, what...what do you think you're doing? Where am I?"

The man laughed.

"Oh, Turvasu. Poor, poor Turvasu. Turvasu the simpleton! Isn't it obvious? You're thirsty, my friend," he laughed.

"Thirsty? What..."

And then the truth dawned on him. He looked behind to see the mighty Sindhu roaring south to the sea.

"No, NO! YOU CAN'T DO THIS...YOU..."

Pipru just laughed.

"Shout all you can, my friend! Nobody can hear you in this abandoned tower!"

Saying so, Pipru toppled Turvasu's chair as he rushed into the stream, ten yards per second.

64

Indra was staring at the fort, trying to work out last-minute threats or weaknesses, when he saw a dark figure falling from the tower.

It's a man!

"Quick, Martand! We need to go there! A man has fallen!"

Martand knew it was urgent. But he realised that helping the enemy before the war? What was the King thinking? Then he realised. They were the Devas. They were gods. On the side of Dharma, even in the worst of times.

They rode on, stopping a little before the site of the tower. The river would have carried off the man with a fast speed.

Sure enough, Indra could see a man on a chair floating downstream. Not caring for his clothes or the cold, he tore off his upper garment and jumped into the freezing Sindhu.

He untied the ropes binding the Brahmin and managed to save him. It took him more than eight minutes to do so, nearly succumbing to pneumonia.

A shivering Indra came out with the unconscious Brahmin boy.

"T-t-t-t-take h-h h-h-himmm..."

Martand followed the orders while Aryaman appeared with a shawl.

"Ansha," he called out to Anshuman.

"Send a letter postponing the peace conference!"

Anshuman rushed off, nodding.

"Come on, my Lord," he said softly.

Indra slowly opened his eyes. His eyes were dilated, and his chest felt warm.

Cannabis. Or wine.

He suddenly noticed a small figure at his feet, clutching a shawl around his chest.

"Namaste, Brahmin," he greeted as he recognised the boy he had just saved.

"Oh, Lord Devendra, you are as great as they say! You even let the Panis live. I come at your feet as a humble servant," he said.

"First of all, stop it. No need to be formal," he said. He was always uncomfortable with compliments, praise and honour.

"No, my Lord. I am but a simple Brahmin. You are the King of The Gods."

Indra sighed.

"I am indebted to you for saving my life. I don't know how to thank you enough."

"By not calling me a 'god'," he smiled.

The boy seemed to be from an orthodox Brahmin family where the rulers were not to be questioned.

"What's your name?"

"Turvasu, Your Highness," replied the boy.

"You braved the waters well, Turvasu. Not bad. Not bad at all."

65

"What? Nine days!" said an astonished Indra.

"Yes, My Lord. And Vangrida has rejected the option of peace," continued Aryaman.

Indra secretly thanked the gods. He would now be remembered as the destroyer of forts.

"Also, one more thing," he continued.

"What?" asked Indra.

"The Rudra wants to meet you."

Indra stared quizzically at him.

"He's in that tent," he pointed to a silk tent surrounded by Bhutagana warriors with a bull banner.

The bull was the symbol of the first Rudra, Lord Sadashiv. Legends say he rode into battle on the back of his favourite aurochs, Lord Nandi. Even today, in temples dedicated to Lord Shiva, a sculpture of Nandi was placed strategically in the temple. He symbolised Dharma, knowledge and devotion.

Indra put on his finest violet silk angavastra and golden dhoti with a blue border. He wore comfortable sandals and took his symbol: a blue banner with a white elephant and a thunderbolt.

He walked into the office tent where Pashupati was waiting. On the way, he also noticed some sadhus who had no banner. Or clothes.

Ignoring the sadhus, a few of whom had now begun to smoke from clay chillums, he strode into the tent.

Three men and one woman were sitting on the comfortable sofas.

The one on the right had his hair rolled into a bun. He had Rudraksh beads around his neck. His leather necklace was shaped exactly like a cobra with an outstretched neck and hood. The ceremonial horned headdress of the Rudra was tucked under his arm.

The woman was dressed in a modest dhoti and simple angavastra. Her lips were painted pink with some fruit extract. Her gold jewellery was quite plain for a woman of her stature.

The third man looked like a king. He was dressed in a white angavastra and white dhoti. His gold crown, earrings and necklace added to his looks. Royal slippers with velvet and gold embroidery covered his feet. An ornately decorated scabbard held an expensive recurved Egyptian sword.

The fourth man, though, was the most intimidating of them all. His bloodshot eyes were the result of cannabis usage, mostly ritual. A tigerskin blanket and red *kaupinyam* were his only clothes. A jute bag hung from a string over his right shoulder. The janeu had been rolled up to his chest for ease of movement. Battle scars gleamed over ribs protruding from ritual fasting.

Ashes covered every inch of his skin, giving him the appearance of a sadhu. His matted bun added seven inches to his normally six-feet-three-inches height. Strings of Rudraksh beads lined his bun. Three horizontal lines of sandal paste and a vertical vermillion line in their centre pledged his loyalty to Lord Shiva. Indra bowed his head and folded his hands, greeting them all individually.

"My apologies for making you wait, Lord Rudra. And may I say that your formation seems impenetrable?" he said, hoping to get into Rudra's good books.

"Not needed, Your Highness. Reinstating Dharma in our country is the only compliment I need. But complimenting my locks would also do!" said Pashupati with a straight face before laughing.

The sadhu-like man rolled his eyes while the King smiled. The woman did not get over the shock of seeing a Deva.

"Uh, allow me to introduce my wife, Ambika; my General, the former King of Indraprastha, Lord Rijishva; and this is," he said, pointing to the Sadhu, "Lord Bhairav Kalaantak, the previous Rudra."

Indra narrowed his eyes.

So, this bastard killed Father.

Bhairav felt Indra's piercing gaze and sighed.

"I keep no secrets," he began.

"I admired your father, boy. But he broke the rules. Dharma is above all. I would rather destroy the Asuras than let someone deceive me into reinstating "good". Destruction is the key! And you know that, don't you?" said Bhairav, referring to Indra's inner desire of being remembered as the destroyer of forts.

His eyes widened.

"How..."

"There are no secrets from a yogi," he answered mysteriously.

Indra felt his legs weaken. If there were no secrets from this man, would he know about the insult?

No! That was a cheap magic trick! Just a random guess! You can't just read minds!

"I don't mind any insults you throw at me! I'm detached from the world. And there are some things possible for a spiritually enlightened soul," he smiled.

Indra's heart beat faster while the assembled people began to stare quizzically at what was now becoming a one-sided, mysterious conversation.

Bhairav gestured with his eyes at Pashupati, and Indra remembered the conversation.

"Right, so…uh…"

"You were about to compliment my locks," said Pashupati to lighten the mood. It did the trick.

"So, anyways, we, the Bhutaganas, have always believed that the Devas are the representatives of Dharma here on the earth. Though they have committed some questionable things in the past, they are still a lot closer to Dharma than the other tribes, say the Yakshas," began Pashupati.

"That is why you are worshipped like gods!"

"And what made you come here to this simple battle camp in the middle of—" Indra's sentence was cut short by loud orders being relayed by the Adityas and clangs of steel.

The Rudra and the Devendra marched out to see the first battle wave.

66

"MARUTS! FORMATION!" shouted Martand while fighting an invader with a demon mask, standard Asura wartime attire.

The Asuras possessed shock troops with frightening visages—during the ancient battles against Lord Vaaman, the Asura King Mahabali had invented an ingenious solution to scare the Deva armies.

Lord Vaaman, the foremost Aditya at twelve, was blessed with the sharpest intellect. Propaganda posters that painted the Asuras as cannibalistic demons were anonymously put up around the Sapta-Sindhu and prevented the other tribes from joining them.

The masks commonly featured violently warm colours, grotesque visages, contorted features, long moustaches and sometimes fangs, with the most ornate being decorated with horn, antler, bone and boar tusk horns.

However, Marut's training required braving hallucinogenic paranormal experiences, which were almost certainly never positive. These men were built for this. The confused Asuras nearly shat their dhotis when they saw their usual tactics failing! With their golden breastplates and superior bronze armour, the thundercloud of Maruts leapt upon the Kalakeyas like a pack of lions on a hapless lamb.

Suddenly, men with silver breastplates and similar build to the Maruts emerged from near the Rudra's tent.

These were Pashupati's bodyguards, the Warriors of Rudra, the Raudras.

"*RUDRASYA MARYAH!*" was their battle cry—the Men of Rudra.

"MARUTAH VIDYUT!" cried the Maruts. *The Maruts are lightning.*

The two identical armies slashed through the back and left of the army, the points of weakness in a phalanx.

It was not a battle. It was two butchers against one lamb.

"Now we have lost all our men!" thundered Vangrida.

Eight hundred men with Vritra, and the rest dead. That left him with a hundred archers and the King of The Devas with practically his entire army.

"The remaining soldiers?" he asked.

"Um, My Lord, ah, but, I uh..."

"Speak up, man!" barked Vangrida.

The man kept staring at his shoes.

"Is...is no one left?" he asked as the gravity of the situation dawned on him.

The man silently nodded.

"NOOO!" he cried as his knees buckled under him.

His sons, Parnaya and Karanja, had been involved in the skirmish. That would mean...

"Which son of a bitch killed them? Find me the bastard's head!" he hissed menacingly.

This was not the king of the Northern Kalakeyas speaking. This was a soul robbed of the reason for its existence. A boat without a captain. A mind without reason. Decisions without logic. Revenge. From a person who had nothing to lose.

The soldiers were inspecting the kills. However, they were working methodically, inspecting the corpses and searching for clues pointing out royal lineage. And sure enough, a few minutes later, they found two corpses.

They were dressed in crimson war clothes. Wooden war masks with their names inscribed in gold letters. Karanja and Parnaya. They had died in the most gruesome manner.

Their bodies had several cuts in different places. Their heads had been smashed in with a mace. Brains— purple and glistening— were splattered all around. The stomach had been kicked repeatedly by a large boot. But, the killing blow was with a spear.

Embossed in ivory was the bearer's name: Indra.

"I shall have that arseface's head! That little shit will die by my hands!" he spat.

General Shambara had the good sense to remain mute.

"I killed that slimeball's father! It's about time I get him."

He had begun crying by now. His wife, Sunctra, glared at him, pure venom reflecting in his eyes. Because of his zeal, she had lost the two biggest pieces of her soul. She had never loved Vangrida anyway.

However, when her sons came, Parnaya and Karanja, she finally thought she knew happiness. But, Vangrida had insisted on sending her sons to a far-away military school to study. They came a decade later. After that, Vangrida sent them for army training. They came back, just in time, unfortunately, for the war.

Now, her life was shattered. Forever.

"Lord Rijishva, we have succeeded. All because of you. The Warriors of Rudra gave us the upper hand in the battle. For that, I thank you. With all my heart, I swear on all the Gods, I accept you as my ally, my brother," said a grateful Indra.

Rijishva's eyes moistened.

"Glory to Lord Devendra!" he roared with all his might.

Indra embraced him like a brother. Just a few decades later, the friendship of Indra and Rijishva would be recounted in the holiest scripture of the Sapta-Sindhu, the Rig Veda.

67

"Archers to their stations!" shouted Shambara.

The hundred archers still left with Vangrida would be put to use in the late-night siege. The Devas were still sleeping. The blood from the last skirmish would be avenged.

"Where is Turvasu?" asked Vangrida. The chief of staff was required at this hour.

Pipru feigned grief.

"A tragedy happened, Your Highness. My dear friend Turvasu died…by drowning!"

He had begun to fake cry by now. Vangrida ignored him and went away. He was beyond caring now. He didn't give a damn about what happened and what did not. All he cared about was vengeance.

"Are the preparations done?" he asked Shambara.

"Your majesty, the archers are assembling. Other than that, everything is ready. Should we burn down the Deva tents?

"NO! I WANT INDRA'S HEAD!"

Shambara wanted to say something but shut up in time. Here was a man who had lost everything. He had lost every ounce of logic, sanity and empathy. He was beyond caring now.

But he couldn't risk the his soldiers' lives. He tried to think of a strategy.

"My lord, why don't we just attack the soldiers' tents when Indra comes out and then you can shoot him?"

Vangrida thought about it.

"Just two tents," he agreed reluctantly.

Shambara secretly thanked the gods for his master's change of mind.

The tents were burning full blaze. It looked as if the Fire God, Lord Agni himself, descended from mid-air to witness the spectacle and join in. The blaze seemed to neutralise the cold winter air with ease. The offending fire arrow lay burning in the blaze, its tip flaming red.

But one curious thing got Vangrida's attention.

"Shambara, why are there no screams? No men seem to run out! What the hell is—"

His sentence was cut short by a humongous projectile soaring with a high velocity and-

BOOM!

It crashed into the tower with a loud roar and sat there hissing. Just before anyone could do anything about it, it exploded into millions of arrow parts, glass pieces and a shower of shrapnel, accompanied by an explosion that would make the Agneyastra lower its eyes in embarrassment.

Within minutes, the fire spread and the Western wall was nearly destroyed.

It was the weapon of the God of the Rains. The rain of arrows; The rains from hell. The Indrastra.

"The western wall has been breached, and only twenty-eight survivors from our side!" panicked Shambara.

Shrapnel and arrowheads had pierced his abdomen. He would not be able to survive much longer. But, his duty bound him to inform his king.

"Take the men to the inner cit—"

A sword was brutally rammed through his back and emerged from his guts, splattering blood, guts and gore on Vangrida's robe. The scimitar was pulled out just as swiftly, and the rasping Shambara kicked out of the way, his punctured lung causing him to spit and cough blood.

From behind the man emerged Rijishva.

"IN THE NAME OF DEVENDRA, BEST AMONG THE DEVAS AND THE BULL AMONG MEN! GLORY TO SHIVA!" he roared as he slashed viciously with his scimitar.

The attack was countered effectively by the use of Vangrida's bow. The sword got stuck into the wood, giving Vangrida enough time to draw out his own scimitar.

"Who are you?" he hissed menacingly.

"You may call me Athithigva, the hospitable host," said Rijishva, referring to his nickname.

The chilly winter air and the sheer intensity of the duel, punctuated by cries of "*Rudrasya Maryah*" and "*Marutah Vidyut*", made it look like an event choreographed by the great War God, Lord Skand himself.

The fight lasted more than twenty minutes. The starting moves from Rijishva were calculated, deliberate and slow. By contrast, Vangrida started energetically but drained himself of energy after a few minutes.

A backhanded move from Athithigva was parried by a sharp stab from Vangrida. Vangrida's sword pierced his thigh as Rijishva hawked and spat in his eye. Vangrida momentarily lost balance and fell to the ground.

Rijishva wasted no time and kicked Vangrida's groin. As the Asura hollered and howled in pain, the bloodied General of the Bhutaganas finished the fight, once and for all, as he pushed the sword into the Kalakeya leader's throat.

Game over.

Turvasu was roaming the Western tower's destroyed portion, which used to serve as the servants' quarter and his old home. As he walked, his eyes fell on a familiar figure charred by the flames. He was still alive and was gasping for breath.

The soot and ash blackened his face. His left leg lay several metres away, severed by the attack. Blood had congealed around his stubble, and his wounds still leaked.

Flies hovered around the wound on his chest, and ravens and vultures were approaching.

Turvasu stiffened as the dying figure of Pipru recognised him.

"Tu...Turva...Help...M-"

The last breath of life escaped his figure as Turvasu was rid of the threat to his life.

68

The contingent of the Devendra and the Rudra was met with outrage from the Kalakeya citizens of the Fort of Lakshman.

"DIE!"

"FIE ON YOUR CLAN!"

"MAY YOU ROT IN *NARAK!*"

"MAY FUNGI INFEST YOUR ARMPITS!"

Ignoring the insults heaped on him and trying not to laugh at the last one, Indra began climbing up the temporary stage set up in the middle of the city square. However, he did not need additional height as he was already on Airavata's back.

He cleared his throat.

"Citizens of Lakhanjo Daro!" he said and paused for a dramatic effect.

The men began to hurl rotten fruit but were abruptly stopped by the raised shields of the Maruts and the Bhutagana soldiers.

"You may be against me. Against the Devas. By birth, you are taught to hate us. Have you ever considered the reason for this? Do any of you know about the truth or its history? We worship the same gods! We eat the same food. We are all human, after all. We can live together. We can all be one."

The men stopped pelting the fruits but were still not convinced. This was it—the time to drive the point home.

"These letters were recovered from your King's private chambers. They are addressed...to the King of the Nivatakavachas!"

A collective gasp emerged from the crowd. The Nivatakavachas? There were rumours that those scum of the earth would willingly sacrifice their children to a goat-headed deity.

"But it's not too late," continued Indra.

"We can defeat evil. The actual evil that has caused the rift. A long time ago, before even the age of Manu, Devas and Asuras were brothers. We were one. Our ancestors were a single tribe. What happened? What caused the rift? Historians may speculate. But whatever happened was bad. We need to unify once again. We can be the Aryas again!"

Arya, meaning a noble or a hero, was a term of respect for warriors or those who contributed to society. Over time, however, its definitions changed. To the Asuras, it meant the racially pure ones. To the rest, those born in "civilised society", not including tribals, were the Aryas.

Arya was a word that could not be used in the context of Asuras. It had been too long since the Asuras had been deprived of what they rightfully deserved. Respect.

Finally, after what seemed like an eternity, the citizens of the Fort of Lakshman genuflected on one knee and bowed their heads, their balled fists raised high into the air. Then they roared in the Language of the Gods.

"INDRAYA VIJAYAH!"

Glory to Indra.

"With the aid of Lord Indra, the men have defeated Vangrida. And the Rudra is coming," said Hiranyastupa, explaining the basic outline of Aryaman's most recent scroll.

Shachi's eyes widened. It was a rare honour that very few women had the privilege of experiencing. The representative of Lord Shiva in her kitchen!

She began to get up, but Prithvi held up an arm to stop her. "You're pregnant. Rest," she ordered.

Shachi smiled. Her mother-in-law was caring. But strict when it came to personal health.

"I'll instruct the maids," she ordered.

Shachi smiled and gazed at her belly. The twins were a week due.

The entry of the Devendra and the Rudra was accompanied by a presentation of military discipline, war trumpets and a demonstration of their military prowess.

"*MARUTAH VIDYUT!*" shouted the Maruts who had stayed behind in the fort.

"*Rudrasya Maryah,*" came the energetic reply.

"Har Har Mahadev!" shouted the inhabitants.

The citizens were ecstatic on seeing their living god.

Indra noticed an unnaturally tall man with powerful musculature and the Deva crown among the assembled crowd. He was dressed in his usual trefoil wrap . The pendant of swan and lotus hung from his gold chain. His greying beard, hair, and battle scars revealed a tough life.

Like Indra's, his usually serious face and eyes now conveyed happiness.

Indra tried to hold back the tears. But the dam burst.

I have avenged you, father, he whispered in the confines of his mind. He heard Dyaus' voice in his head.

Do not avenge me. Avenge your motherland, my motherland, our motherland.

Saying so, he turned away, and Indra was shaken out of his reverie by Mitra, pointing to the show of friendly competition and swordsmanship between the Maruts and Rudra's guards.

I shall avenge the Sapta-Sindhu.

69

"How the hell did they buy that?!" asked an incredulous Nasatya, who had not been present at Indra's speech.

"Yes, I mean, first he says, 'Hey, we have to be all friendly, we are all the same', and the next second he just blames the Nivatakavachas and then promotes Arya supremacy," explained Mitra.

"I would not have put it that way," smiled Indra as Shachi chuckled.

"By the gods, I missed you," said Indra, embracing Shachi.

The formal demeanour had to be maintained until Prithvi went away.

"I missed you too," said Shachi, kissing Indra on the forehead.

"I can't wait for cousins to play with!"

Vashishth had just entered the room unannounced.

"Come here!" said Mitra, dragging him into a bear hug.

"Oh, come on! Dad, you stink! Go take a bath," he said, crinkling his nose.

Mitra sniffed his armpits and pretended to be intoxicated and happy. Vashishth gagged. Everyone laughed.

"So, even the Bhutaganas are fed up with the Asuras?" Indra asked Pashupati.

"More than you can imagine."

"And the waters?"

"Are still being held by Vritra. The dams really seem to be holding up. They seem to be indestructible. Even the rains are not falling," added Pashupati.

"And what other issues does your tribe face in the Sapt-Sindhu?"

"Well, the waters, the rains, Asura oppression, censorship, abolition of free speech and human trafficking. And territory dispute. These three Asura brothers have this Citadel and can flood the Sindhu anytime. The city is at risk."

Indra nodded.

"We might need Divyastras against them. Something new. I have heard there are spies amongst us. It must be secret."

Indra nodded.

"I understand. Lord Hiranyastupa?"

"I will uh…do some experiments, uh…" he looked a bit nervous.

Indra eyed him suspiciously as he hurried off.

Strange.

Indra shrugged off the feeling as he saw Shachi in the hospital.

The Royal Hospital of Mehrgarh was the building's official title. It was built two hundred years after an earthquake damaged the previous building.

Built in the traditional circular Asura style, the building resembled a typical Pani home, except it was a lot larger. Three stories tall, the building was spread over at least one acre. One hundred rooms lined the building. An unusual thing that was distinct here from the other unorganised Asura tribes was the discipline.

Cleaning staff wore black, doctors white, nurses yellow, midwives pink and patients brown or ochre. After the battle of Mehrgarh, Indra anonymously donated fifteen thousand gold mudras to the hospital. Fresh coats of the calming white paint had been spread over the earlier peeling yellow .

Gardens had replaced the slum tents, whose brainwashed inhabitants were now languishing in jails.

The Pani administration had successfully promoted the ideas of hatred towards Devas, which would lead to a boosting economy. The rich reacted with indifference—the poor with agreement.

The hospital was the place where Shachi was admitted right now.

Her bed was placed in one of the premium rooms with a window-side view. She was sixteen hours due. She greeted everyone with a smile. But a nagging question came back like the devil to bite her.

Will the delivery be successful? No! Shachi, push these thoughts away!

Ambika had, earlier in the day, come to meet her. She carried new clothes, gold jewellery and even toys as gifts.

"Thank you," said a grateful Shachi.

"No need to than me. It's a ritual so the new mother doesn't fret over dresses and gold. Also, to show how rich I am," joked Ambika, and the women laughed.

Pashupati rolled his eyes outside in the corridor.

Women.

Women, indeed.

Indra was standing beside the bedside table, holding Shachi's hand.

"Shh! Relax! Everything's going to be fine," he said.

Labour pain had not yet begun, but the midwife said it would start within the hour.

"All right."

Shachi allowed herself to calm down.

"My lord, the spy has come,"

Vritra was in his private study, scrolls of vellum lining his desk. He sighed.

"Let him in. And please, he has a name."

The servant nodded apologetically and rushed out. The short, hooded man walked in.

"Well, well, well! Look who it is! From serving the Angiras to now being the Devendra's right-hand man! You've come a long way," he said as the man removed his mask.

70

"AAH!"

Shachi hollered in pain as the midwife tugged at the first child.

"Come on, come on, My Lady. Breathe, HARDER!"

Shachi exhaled deeply, and the first child slipped out. Wasting no time, the midwife signalled the other one and swiftly cut the child's umbilical cord. She then wiped the amniotic fluid and wrapped the baby in the towel. She handed over the child to Indra.

"My Lord, it's a girl," she smiled.

Indra's eyes watered as he held his progeny for the first time. His daughter, his own flesh and blood.

On the other side of the room, the midwives were busy trying to safely extract the second child. Shachi was bravely trying to stay awake and endured the pain bravely. Out slipped the second child.

Finally, the midwives presented Indra with his second baby.

"A girl and a boy, my Lord. The gods have indeed blessed you. I tell you, conceiving both a boy and a girl is not easy, that too in one pregnancy!" said the chatty, extroverted midwife. Indra gave her a pouch of fifty gold mudras as a reward.

She graciously accepted the pouch and held it to her forehead as a thank you to the gods.

Shachi smiled weakly towards Indra and closed her eyes before instantaneously falling asleep. She finally saw a girl whom Indra loved more than his wife.

The royal astrologer had calculated the movements of the planets, the lunar house and the solar house to list auspicious consonants to name the child. Since the planetary positions for both children were the same, the auspicious letters were *bha*, *chha* and *ja*. Indra already had a name decided. Jayant. The victorious. The daughter was named Jayanti.

According to a popular Deva tale, the daughter of the third Devendra, Lord Purandar, Lady Jayanti, was one of the most beautiful women to have ever lived. Men worshipped the ground she walked upon.

However, she did not care for any of those love-stricken Cupids and instead had a fancy for the Asura High Priest. The Asura High Priests were named Shukracharya after Lord Mahabali's Guru, who established the Asura Constitution. The Shukracharya was the highest authority on all Asura matters, and all the Asura tribes, including the Nivatakavachas, followed his order. She secretly meant to meet her lover, defying the laws.

She finally convinced the Shukracharya to sign a proclamation saying the Deva and Asuras were allies. She managed to end the border skirmishes that were burdening the empire financially.

Jayant and Jayanti. The progeny of the God of Thunder.

10 YEARS LATER

71

Three swift military campaigns had taken place after the victory over the Fort of Lakshman. The Western banks of the Sindhu were now official Deva territory. Mohenjo-Daro continued to remain an ally. The Sindhu dam could not be destroyed, as per the Rudra's treaty, which included the Devas.

Indra had finally decided to settle down after years of battle. He wanted to watch his children grow up. He was out hunting with Nasatya, Dasra, Jayant and Jayanti. The twins had been promoted to the rank of Ashwin. Two Ashwins were critical for the standard Deva strategies involving two flanks of cavalry.

"Dad! Look, a tiger!" whispered Jayanti.

Tigers were uncommon but not rare in these parts of the Sapt-Sindhu. Usually preferring deep rainforests or grasslands, tigers were one of the few felines that could survive in any environment.

Jayant stared at the beast, his mouth wide open, eyes gleaming excitedly. Dasra looked up at the howdah on Airavata's back and noticed the young boy's expressions. He nudged Indra and pointed to the howdah where the twins were sitting.

"You want it, son?" whispered Indra.

Jayant nodded from above.

Indra readied his bow and was about to nock an arrow when Jayant hissed.

"No!"

Indra looked up, surprised.

"I want it alive," he said.

Indra raised an eyebrow, and Jayant whispered.

"In a cage."

Indra thought. The arrow was the only way to trap the tiger. Nets couldn't be prepared now, of all times. It would be a tedious hunt. Not to mention the issue of bringing the tiger back to the fort.

Nasatya eagerly pointed to the appropriately sized chariot, which could be used to accommodate the beast.

"But how do we render it unconscious? We can't just carry a tiger without getting it to sleep!"

"Sedatives?" suggested Dasra.

"In the middle of nowhere. Yeah, right," Indra rolled his eyes sarcastically.

"I've got some in my satchel," suggested Nasatya.

"And, pray tell, how do we administer an oral-induced sedative into the tiger's body?"

"We could lace some meat with the medicine."

Indra was about to retort when he saw a goat carcass at the tiger's feet.

If we drive it away for a few moments, we might drop some of the drug and run...

The hunt was on.

Tvashtri was searching anxiously for the king of the Devas. His pilgrimages had become more and more frequent, visiting once a year to Southern Aryavarta to the Tirumala temple.

One of the grandest and finest temples in the entire subcontinent, the Tirumala temple was dedicated to the Great God, Lord Narayana himself, worshipped in idol form.

Southern Aryavarta was the only place where there was no trace of Asuras. The Kalakeya supremacy could not reach south of the Narmada. Brahmin clans, martial in nature and claiming descent from Lord Parshuram managed to safeguard the Vedic traditions.

These sages were led by the supreme authority of the Brahmins in Southern Aryavarta; the Agastya. A title passed down to the most accomplished rishi in the South, it was the Agastya's duty to pass on his skills to his disciples.

Silambam, the traditional Aryavarta sport of stick-fighting. Lore said it was invented by Lord Parshuram who could fight both with his axe-head and the shaft.

Tvashtri visited three temples on his annual pilgrimage. The Somanath temple in Saurashtra, the Vishwanath temple in Kashi and the Tirumala Tirupati temple.

Temples in the Asura empire were taxed. Priests, donation boxes and pilgrims were milked dry in the process of absolute dominance. Scriptures could only be read in a fix time, that too after midnight. This meant absolute ban as Vedic rites could only be performed in the day.

The only group left untouched by Vritra were the Sadhus, who lived in ritual poverty, even renouncing clothes. No point taxing them. Truth be told, Vritra was a bit scared of the Sadhus who, he had heard, possessed mystical and supernatural powers.

It usually took about two months for Tvashtri's pilgrimage to finish. And to prove to the gods his loyalty to Brihaspati's mission. Folklore of the local tribes suggested that Lord Tirupati was witness to all activities of the Universe.

Right now, however, Tvashtri was in the city and had an ill-feeling about the hunt.

He was pacing to-and-fro in the forge when Bhairav entered.

"He's in trouble," he whispered cryptically before rushing out.

Tvashtri grabbed the nearest shawl and rushed out, intent on saving his king's life. For the mission. The mission that could save Aryavarta.

72

The bait lay in the sand. It was time to check whether the beast had taken the bait. Distracting the feline with a magnificent show of archery, the tiger took up the bait and chased the noise of Dasra's horse, which was used to distract the tiger.

Once it reached close enough—

WHOOSH! SLICE!

The arrow scared the cat, and it ran away. Taking the opportunity, he added the odourless drug used to treat sick horses and ran away, covering his scent with mud.

All that was left now was to wait.

"Dad! Dad!"

Jayant whispered as he shook the sleeping Indra. The long wait bored Indra, who was now napping.

"Huh…um…erm, Yes, I'm awake!" he said.

Jayanti rolled her eyes.

Boys!

The creature looked magnificent in the moonlight, eating the dead antelope, its fur gleaming in sharp contrast to the landscape.

Jayant's eyes widened. Indra kept observing the beast, waiting for signs of lethargy to creep in. Sure enough, fifteen minutes later, the beast began to get drowsy. It sat on the ground, seemingly full of the meagre food it had eaten as a tiger.

It began to yawn as if it was drunk. Another quarter of an hour, and the beast lay unconscious on the floor.

"Hurry! Tie it down. We leave for the fort. Now."

The boys nodded as they set to work. The tiger was tied down and put into the chariot, legs folded.

Tvashtri whipped his horse into action. He had briefly stopped to rest. He kicked the horse, and it burst into a brisk trot.

"Faster, you dumbass!" growled Tvashtri.

He had to reach the king in time.

Jayant and Jayanti were fighting again.

"Stop pulling my hair!" she shouted.

"I was just saying it looks different!" Jayant responded.

"So, what?"

"That means you are adopted." He grinned.

Jayanti smacked him. "I'm older than you!"

"By two minutes."

"So that means I am not adopted."

Jayant sighed.

It was not easy to defeat her in a verbal duel. Her choice of words was better and more refined than other girls her age.

Indra smiled at Jayanti.

"I went easy on her. I let her win," interjected Jayant.

"Sure you did," said Jayanti, rolling her eyes.

Indra chuckled heartily, remembering his carefree childhood days and Mitra's taunts.

Life was beautiful then.

73

The beast woke up, its nostrils sniffing the air around it. It noticed its tied-up paws. A simple jute rope held together with a simple twist knot. It stretched its paws with the speed of a swift and wrenched apart the ropes. Thankfully, the Ashwins did not notice. The hind legs were not tied but simply folded.

The beast stood up and shook its fur. It growled, and Dasra turned back to look, mortified at the scene's horror. The tiger leapt upon the boys. The boys would surely have been maimed if it were not for their battle training.

"Lord Devendra!"

The five Marut guards that were accompanying the Devendra for protection instantly dismounted and pointed their weapons at the hulking beast of three hundred kilograms. The tiger growled at the circle of men around it.

"MARUTAH VIDYUT!"

The battle cries alerted Indra. He jumped off Airavata ten feet into the sand.

"Sword!" he ordered.

Nasatya obliged. He handed his scimitar and removed his bow from his back.

The Maruts retreated into standard turtle formation, shields out front, and Indra unsheathed his sword. The gleam of steel was reflected in the tiger's eyes.

"NASATYA, TAKE AWAY THE CHILDREN! MARUTS! BLOCK PATH! BEHIND ME!"

A father's top priority during the conflict was to ensure his children's protection. This could even be seen in the wild when a lion sent away his pride to fight the rival.

The Lion among Men thus ensured his children's protection as he threw the scabbard and unhooked his shield. The sword was one of the sharpest in the Deva armies. Unfortunately, the tiger did not know that.

It lunged at the man and sunk its claws into the right forearm. The sword fell from his arm, and the shield pressed in deeper as Indra cried out in pain.

The numbness in his brain drowned out the war cry of "Jai Agni" from the lone rider, Tvashtri, as he plunged his longsword into the tiger's abdomen. Blood spluttered from its mouth and gut as life slipped from the creature's body.

Before losing consciousness, Indra saw the concern on Tvashtri's face as Jayanti came crying into Indra's arms.

74

The Kalakeya War Council sat in stony silence. The recent scroll from the Angira mole said the last fort under Kalakeyas' dominion had fallen. The Asura generals observed silence, honouring the men who had lost their lives, bravely fighting to the last man.

It was good that everyone perished. The new Deva policy of brainwashing the Asuras by his "Arya" concept. He couldn't risk sending more men to Indra.

"What be our next course of action?" asked General Shushna.

"We can't send more men, Lord Shushna. With all due respect, our men are outnumbered. The sheer number of Asuras on the side of the Devas; we'll be lucky if our men don't revolt by the monsoon," said an agitated Anha.

A hot-headed bald man of fifty, love handles emerged above his usually low-tied dhoti. The Asura Treasurer's opulent lifestyle was quite evident from his paunch. A blue angavastra with polka-dot designs was casually thrown over his shoulders. Clusters of hair lined his chest, armpits, navel, and even ears. A veteran who had survived internal conflicts among the Kalakeya tribes, Anha would often thank the gods that he had found Vritra, a charismatic leader, genius strategist, and unifier of the Kalakeya Clans.

"The mole said the King trusts him with his life," smiled Vritra.

The assembled men laughed. It was time for an assassination.

75

Indra felt soft hands on his cheeks. He also felt the thick stubble.

How long have I been like this?

He felt someone force open his mouth and put a wooden ladle of some sort of soup.

Mm...my favourite!

He gently opened his eyes to find Jayanti blowing on another spoonful of soup.

"You're awake?" she asked gleefully.

"Yes. How long have I..."

"A week," said Shachi, who had just entered.

"Good morning," he wished her.

She smiled.

"How was your beauty nap?"

"Couldn't have been better," he smiled.

Mitra and Varuna entered, Jayant on Mitra's shoulders.

Indra stared at the boy.

It's just been one week, and he's already forgotten me!

He smiled.

"Jayant," he called softly.

Mitra put him down, and Jayant ran to his father.

"Father! Father! Look what I have drawn!" he said, showing a piece of paper to Indra.

On it was a simple childish drawing of an armoured man fighting an orange and black…

Not to hurt the boy's feelings, he observed the drawing. The boy's attention to detail was way too advanced for his age, even though it was a fattened stick figure. The knuckle-bow of the sword had been replicated, the cut on Indra's brow and even the colour of the shoe leather. Marut guards, represented as yellow-chested stick figures, held shields high.

"By the gods! This is a masterpiece, man!" he praised.

Happily, Jayant pulled out a wooden sword from his waistband. He held it to Indra's chest, who retorted by using the fruit plate as a shield, throwing two peaches on the floor.

Boys, after all, Jayanti sighed.

"I hope you're well, my Lord," said Hiranyastupa as he walked in.

"Never been better," said Indra, putting down the manuscript in his hands. Jayanti rolled her eyes and put a bookmark in the inverted book.

"Where is Tvashtri, Lord Hiranyastupa?"

"My Lord, his pilgrimage."

Indra nodded.

"And the new Astras I told you to experiment with?"

"My Lord, we have experimented with the Somaras and its combustibility. My assistant, Kutsa, shall tell you more details. Kutsa, if you may," said Hiranyastupa, looking at the young man near him.

"Namaste, Your Highness. I am Kutsa, Hiranyastupa Ji's assistant. I have done extensive research on the Soma's astra-making capabilities. And, these are my findings."

Kutsa looked no older than twenty-eight. He had a *tilak* on his forehead and long-shoulder-length hair. He wore a saffron vest, red sash, and white dhoti. He carried a small satchel from which he extracted palm leaves held together with string. Unbeknownst to most, he had even practised Shastra Vidya, warcraft.

Indra studied the report. It showed a diagram of some kind of an astra with the regular arrow shape and the cylinder filled with the weapon.

The next page showed a cross-section of the cylinder. The outside was labelled iron, and the inside was filled with a liquid. Soma paste mixed with ghrita.

The next page described its construction, operation, and mechanism. Sanskrit verses described the weapon's potency. The uniqueness of this weapon—one spark and it would begin to heat up. The Soma, unstable before adding milk, would result in an orange explosion capable of removing entire mountains.

"Brilliant," beamed Indra.

The war begins!

76

Facing the river at Lakhanjo Daro, which had now been renamed Lakshmandurg again, was a temple to Lord Ram.

The temple complex housed four temples. The centre one was dedicated to Lord Ram; the one on its left to Lady Sita, his wife, who was always placed to his left, his heart. The one on the right was dedicated to Lord Lakshman, Lord Ram's brother and right-hand man.

And the one on the gate to Lord Hanuman, the dearest companion, eternal servant, and most fervent devotee of Lord Ram, the Avatar. The strongest among the Vaanars, Lord Hanuman was also the most skilled from the monkey tribe. Well-versed in Sanskrit, Prakrit, mace warfare, swordsmanship, archery, music, wrestling, and even Vimana-flying, Lord Hanuman was said to be an immortal, still roaming the highlands of Kimpurusha territory.

After his daily bath, Indra put on an angavastra and walked to the temple. Removing his sandals at the door, he climbed the ten stairs to walk into the temple complex. He first visited the temple of Lord Hanuman and offered his prayers.

The idol was built of granite and was covered in vermillion. Lord Hanuman was dressed in a red *kaupinyam* holding a gada, the traditional mace style. A tail emerged from his lower back. He had set fire to the Lankan fortress with the very same tail.

Indra ceremonially placed a laddoo of gram flour in front of the idol as an offering to the Lord.

He then sat for some time, prayed, and emerged from the side door. Now, he went to the temple of Lord Lakshman. His statue was said to be life-sized, reaching a staggering height of six feet and eight inches.

His hand held a bow, and the other held an arrow, ready for action. As in most temples, the vestments of the gods were changed daily. Today, Lord Lakshman was dressed in a yellow dhoti and green angavastra. A replica of his actual bow was also kept on a low table near the seat of the Head Priest.

A composite recurve by design, the massive bow of five feet was said to be the First Nagaraj, Lord Adi Shesha's. Though just a replica, the bow would have induced fear into the hearts of those who beheld it. A bow of this size would also require tremendous force. Judging by the muscles of the Lord's idol, he did not seem to lack it.

These kinds of bows required stabilising by holding one end under a foot and working best only from a high platform, the archers lying on their backs.

Indra offered his prayers and again went away, this time to Lord Ram's temple.

A loud whirring sound was heard before he could even enter the temple. Out of nowhere, a fireball appeared on the horizon. And it was heading straight for the temple.

"RUN!" shouted Indra.

At such an early hour, only the priests were present. No civilians. The priests rushed out to see the commotion. The fireball nearly landed when Indra pushed the priests outside. The fireball was coming straight for Lord Hanuman's temple. Indra rushed through the side door to alert the priest when he saw the ball land a few miles outside the city.

HISSS...

An eerie hiss accompanied the fireball as it drowned in the river.

"Thank Lord Hanuman! Now, get out!" cried Indra.

The priests and Indra ran for their lives. Another loud whirring sound was heard out of nowhere, and another fireball appeared. This time, it wouldn't miss.

Indra was walking in the wreckage of the once beautiful temple complex. The splendid gardens, the rosewater fountain, the splendid marble tiles, the teak carvings; all was gone.

The brunt of the blow was taken by the temple of Lord Hanuman and partially by that of Lord Lakshman. The houses of Lord Ram and Lady Sita, the Daughter of the Earth, bore not a single scratch. The priests called it a miracle of the Lord as only a short while earlier, a macaque was seen drinking some water from the pitcher outside Lord Ram's temple. The water had been specially consecrated and was put out for animals.

Indra went livid as he saw the corpses of two innocent Brahmins, caught by surprise.

He stormed out, rushing off to find the Adityas. It was officially war.

"My Lord, I meant to tell you, but news just came in yesterday, and some of the major Pani leaders escaped and caused a riot in another temple five miles to the southwest. And even the Pani leaders in jails are cursing our gods," said Aryaman.

Indra stared gravely at the map. There were no Kalakeya territories on the Western banks of the Sindhu. Which only meant one thing.

"They're coming from the Eastern side of the Sindhu."

Mitra put into words what everyone's gut felt.

"Which city was responsible for this, though?"

Indra stared at the map. The city had to be close, just opposite Lakshmandurg. It had to be filled with religious fanatics and preferably led by someone...militaristic or charismatic or having a high religious post.

The place seemed obvious. Kotidwija, the city of ten million Aryas, was the city's old name. The Gandharva term, however, was Kot Diji. Earlier a hub of spiritual knowledge, the city was now overrun by Kalakeyas.

The city was home to the Shukracharya. Hence, the fanatics.

"Talk to the Rudra. We attack Kotidwija," said Indra.

Aryaman stared at the map. The answer was obvious. It was the closest fort to Lakshmandurg.

"Brilliant," he grinned.

For too long, the Devas endured religious persecution. Now, it was time for revenge—an eye for an eye.

77

Pyrolatry, or fire worship, was among the oldest forms of worshipping God. For as long as there had been fire, there had been safety. And danger. The fire was the perfect element to call a god. It was capricious, it was mysterious, it needed offerings, it required respect, it was violent, it was benevolent, it protected, and it caused danger. It was…well, fiery.

Almost every culture, even the monotheistic ones, found something godly in fire. Even the Asuras, popularly projected as atheists, surrendered to the flames.

It was the best and most natural representation of Lord Shiva to the Kalakeyas and a signal to the God of the Nivatakavachas. The Danavas even went as far as to worship Lord Agni as the fire's name, not the warrior's.

The fire was originally known as *anala* in Sanskrit. But, after Lord Agni, fire was rechristened as Agni in his honour. Anala, the element, and Agni, the Lord.

The Eternal Flame was one thing that the Asuras couldn't lose at any cost. It was an ancient meteorite that fell nearly five hundred years ago. Unbeknownst to anyone, the flaming meteorite had pierced an underground natural gas pocket. And for five hundred years, that place had been burning. The then-Shukracharya went into a meditative trance and proclaimed the place as the Earth's centre. And that Lord

Shiva had declared in his trance to build a temple for him with neither idol nor image and that the flame shall be the only thing they shall worship.

Hypothetically speaking, if the meteorite were to be removed from the crater, the flame would continue to burn. This was not the case if it were doused.

The flames had often been doused with water, only to get reignited. Before the Shukracharya's prediction, the meteorite was proclaimed evil and repeatedly tried to be doused with water. But there seemed to be some substance in the meteorite that prevented it from getting doused.

Each time, it was doused out; the next morning, it was found in its full splendour.

But if the meteorite were removed, there would be no more flame and no God. It was simple psychological warfare. You take away the enemy's source of strength, his pride, his joy, in this case, his god, and lower his morale. Half the battle is already won!

More than five centuries later, the Hellenic armies would use the same tactics to steal the Palladium from the Trojans. Exiled Asuras and their mighty war elephants would join forces to defend the Trojan King, Priam.

The Deva armies in the war room sat in the War Tent and discussed tactics.

"We need secrecy. Only one soldier must go. And we need fireproof armour," began Indra.

"I know a man, my Lord," said Anshuman as he walked in.

"You're late," said Indra sternly.

"What if you're early?" he joked.

Indra shook his head.

Anshuman sat at the table.

"Speak."

"Matarishvan. He is one of the finest Maruts I have ever known. He is as fast and agile as the wind. He can easily slip in and out with ease. And he knows the language. He can disguise."

Indra knew Matarishvan. The boy was talented. A former pickpocket in the streets of Mehrgarh, Indra took pity on the boy and conscripted him into the army. The only reason he agreed was that the state would now legally take care of his mother and three sisters.

"All right. And the second?"

"The second would merely be used as a lookout. He will act not knowing the thief and would add a distraction for our man to get away."

"Who can do this?" asked Indra.

"Bhrigu of the Angiras," said Anshuman, a glint in his eyes.

78

The mysterious, hooded man was back again for his visit to the capital of the Asuras. He had begun to go to the Sapta-Sindhu regularly to report the happenings of the Devas. The passport provided to him by the Asura government meant that he could legally stay in any Asura town free of cost.

The camel he was riding had gradually grown weak over the years. It was ancient, the exact age unknown to the owner himself. But, it faced every challenge thrown on it by life bravely.

The man, too, had grown weak from worry. The fear of discovery loomed over his head like a giant vulture, witnessing the tiger's hunt by circling above. Alternatively, his own preceptor had begun to question his loyalty to the mission.

But he remained strong and hoped for the Lord to improve everything.

He knocked on the gate of the Citadel, built separate from the city, in a specific three-step code that was known only to the guards and him.

A few minutes later, the door was opened, and two guards removed his mask to check him. They tried to search him for weapons, but he held up a palm to stop them. He then extracted a scroll signed by The Firstborn of the Dragons, permitting him to enter the city, weapons intact.

The guards decided to let him go and closed the door as he went in.

The camel rode on for one hundred and fifty metres to reach the palace. The rider tied the camel to a pole meant to tie horses and removed his sandals before entering. Vritra was in the hallway itself.

"I hope you've succeeded," said Vritra curtly.

No greetings, no formalities. Straight to the point.

"The Devendra trusts me with his life, My Lord," said Tvashtri as he removed his veiled turban.

79

The plan had been set in motion. The attack would take place twenty-five days from now. The temple would be empty for the night due to superstitions surrounding the meteorite on a new moon night. Bhrigu would distract the people with the act of a Tantric. Though a Brahmin, he had some experience of Tantra, training from a Guru in his early twenties.

He would come off as a Yogi from the farthest reaches of Kimpurusha territory, north of the Himalayas. He would use chemicals to create explosions, colour changes, and pretend to go into an oracular trance.

Meanwhile, Matarishvan would secretly break into the temple with special fireproof gloves to extract the meteorite. Bhrigu's distractions would mesmerise the audience while Matarishvan ran out of the city.

Once outside, he would fire a small explosive into the air, a cue for Bhrigu to leave.

It was a foolproof plan with no room for error.

In the forge, Bhrigu was practising his act.

"O, Commander of the natural and unnatural spirits, I invoke you with all the Ghosts, O the one with the matted locks! Enter the fire, O Bhutapati, O Lord of Ghosts, Mahakaal!" he said in a deep baritone, unlike his usual voice.

"Is that the best you can do? Come on! Add something mysterious, something creepy," said Pushan.

Bhrigu thought for a while.

"I know! Why don't I control snakes?"

"Well, can you?" asked a sceptical Pushan.

"I've got twenty-six days, Lord Pushan. Lord Bhairav can train me. But I won't do venomous snakes," he added as an afterthought.

"We're going to Mohenjo-Daro tomorrow. Ask him yourself," said Pushan, leaving Bhrigu to practice.

Matarishvan was in the gymnasium. Clad in just a red kaupinyam, he was practising for the mission to lay ahead. Focussing on overall strength development, he used swords, clubs, and daggers and even wrestled.

There were four types of wrestling in Aryavarta. The first, Hanumanti. Named after Lord Hanuman, this style focussed on technical superiority.

The second was Jambuvanti. Named after Jambuvant, the leader of the Riksha Vaanars during Lord Ram's time, this style focussed on locking and holding the opponent into "bear hugs".

The third was Jarasandhi. This style was named after Jarasandh, the Magadhan King who was the opponent of Lord Krishna and the Pandavas and focussed on breaking the enemy's limbs and joints.

The last was Bhimaseni. This style, named after Lord Bhima, the third Pandava brother, focussed on sheer strength.

Training in all these styles in only twenty-seven days was no mean feat. His routine for each day before the mission was twelve hours of training and eight hours of sleep. The rest of the time was spent reading personal combat techniques from centuries-old war manuals whose tactics would continue to work even four millennia after the deeds of Indra.

It was Indra's first visit to the Rudra's city. Mohenjo-Daro was built in an octagonal shape. Over the years, extra bastions replaced destroyed walls, and the shape was quite distorted. Though extremely advanced for its time, it was evident that the fortress was declining.

Nevertheless, all the men were taken in by the grandeur of the Fort of Manu. Just like most Sapta-Sindhu cities, Mohenjo-Daro was divided into two parts—the Citadel, home to the Rudra and his most important aides, and the Lower City.

The first one housed the Great Pillared Hall containing Rudra's audience chamber, a watch tower and a defence tower occupied by Bhutagana snipers.

The Citadel was arranged in two parts. The first housed the temple of Shiva, the college, the granary, and the Great Bath. Used solely for ritual baths, its outside wall held an inscription. It read-

The Great Bath of Rudra. Built by the Devendra, Dyaus.

Indra felt his eyes water as he stared at the statue of Dyaus that had been placed outside the bath. Built of soapstone, the sculptor definitely took inspiration from the portrait in

Prithvi's hut. His gold crown, beard, hair and trefoil shawl were perfectly created.

I shall avenge the wrongs done to the Devas, father.

Indra whispered in the confines of his mind.

The party marched on to the Palace of Rudra in Pillared Hall. The palace was located behind the hall. It was seven storeys tall and had twenty rooms. It housed the Rudra and his wife, Ambika. In one of the additional rooms meant for guests was Bhairav studying the positions of the heavens.

Rijishva rushed out as soon as he heard the footsteps.

"Lord Devendra!" he shouted with delight. It had been too long.

"It is nice to meet you, Rijishva. I see why they call you Athithigva, the hospitable one," smiled Indra.

"My Lord, I don't go by that name anymore. I am Divodas, Servant of the Devas."

"You're not a servant! You're my best friend," said Indra, dragging him into a bear hug.

80

"O Kapardin, the one with the matted locks—" began Bhrigu.

"No!" barked Bhairav.

"What? I even added the smoke effects," protested Bhrigu.

"Boy, if you want to train from me, do not question me! Understood?" growled Bhairav threateningly as Bhrigu nodded.

"Good. Now, you need to add a little more menace to the growl. Like this. Ahem. O, Kapardin of the matted locks, hear my prayer this night of the dead moon, O Bhutapati. Om Hum Phat Shivaya Swaha!" The last Mantra was louder than the low growl that emerged from his throat until now.

"Whoa," said a seriously impressed Bhrigu. Bhairav couldn't help but smile.

"Shall we try it again? This time with the snake."

Bhrigu nodded nervously. He had still not gotten used to the sensation of having a reptile crawling over him, even though it was not poisonous.

Bhairav had affectionately named the serpent Virupaksha. A Dhaman by species, Virupaksha resembled a cobra. Typical of its species who pretended to be cobras to avoid predators.

Bhairav added the powder to the flames, which crackled and burst dangerously, producing a cloud of grey smoke.

"O Kapardin of the matted locks, hear my prayer on this the night of the dead moon. I summon you, O Bhutapati, with all the ghosts and goblins. Om Hum Phat Shivaya Swaha!" he chanted as the Dhaman began to climb over his arm to hang around his neck.

Bhairav nodded in appreciation as Bhrigu sighed.

"Phew!"

Sweat beads had begun to form on his forehead. It took him a lot of self-restraint not to jump back from the crawl of the snake.

"This time with the ashes," said Bhairav.

The ashes were rubbed all over some Yogis' bodies to remind them of life's impermanence, and that the remainder of everything is ashes.

Bhairav pulled some ashes from his satchel and put them on a tray in a pile as Bhrigu began applying them slowly.

The Rudra's palace had a private boxing ring and even a gymnasium. Matarishvan was swinging viciously with the *mausala* club. Made solely of iron in the shape of a gigantic pestle, the mausala was said to be the weapon of choice of Lord Balaram when wrestling. He was famous for his war plough and his short temper. The club were also renowned.

Indra entered the gymnasium to see Matarishvan practice on dummies.

"Need some help there?" he asked helpfully.

Taken by surprise, Matarishvan dropped the club and turned back.

"Oh, Lord Devendra!"

"I do not doubt your agility. But you may need some help in the physical strength."

"Thanks for the offer, My Lord."

Indra nodded, and a professional wrestler entered.

"This is Arun. He is the finest wrestler in Mohenjo-Daro."

Built like a bull, the balding Arun had a long, curled handlebar moustache like most men of Aryavarta. He nodded to the Marut as Matarishvan cleared the arena.

Arun descended into the arena. Ignoring the opponent, he bent down to apply the sand to his forehead as a mark of respect. He then went to the small altar common in most wrestling arenas across Aryavarta. The idol of Lord Hanuman, decorated with red vermillion and clad in a saffron kaupinyam, was holding a mausala in his hand. The Lord's crown was decorated with silver leaf. His tail emerged from behind the loincloth and curled midway in a position that showed aggression, will to fight and mode of action.

Lord Nataraj, the idol of the second Rudra, was placed to Lord Hanuman's right. Nataraj literally meant Lord of Dance. The Rudras had their birth names. But most often, they were known by their titles. History tended to record the more glorious titles than the birth names.

An excellent dancer and an even better warrior, Lord Nataraj was never said to be inactive. Whether dancing, fighting or other physical activities, Lord Nataraj was always involved in physical activity.

It could be said that the Rajas Guna was his dominant side. That was why he was worshipped by all those needing motivation for physical activity.

Arun bowed to the gods and took their blessings before fighting.

"So, what style of combat suits you, young man?" he asked genially.

"Any," he answered.

Arun nodded and slapped his thighs. He then arranged his arms in a typical wrestler stance and lunged at Matarishvan. Matarishvan dodged the attack and rolled from under his legs. He then jumped on his back and twisted the wrestler's arm. Arun momentarily lost his balance and fell to the ground. Matarishvan pinned him and extracted the sheathed dagger tucked into his kaupinyam.

"Checkmate," he smiled.

Arun smiled.

"You win some, you lose some. But if you can defeat me, no bastard is going to survive a match with you."

Indra applauded loudly.

"Well done, Matarishvan."

Matarishvan got what he wanted—the appreciation of his master.

81

Indra's face was contorted in a mixture of shock and fury. Troubling evidence had emerged. A maid was cleaning Tvashtri's room when she saw a dhoti on the ground. It looked as if the man directly removed it quickly, not even bothering to untuck it or remove the waistband. In the waistband lay a letter addressed to the Firstborn of the Dragons.

Having a good sense of realising the gravity of the situation and keeping her mouth shut, the maid dragged the letter straight to General Aryaman. In the gymnasium, Aryaman did not even bother to clothe himself and ran to Indra in just the Kaupinyam.

Indra read the letter as his face drained of colour. Tvashtri was describing the battle positions used by Indra in the previous battles. Aryaman quietly removed a tablecloth and hastily tied a sarong.

"When is he coming?" Indra asked, eyes blazing with fury.

"A week at best," replied Aryaman. Indra nodded.

82

It was the day of the mission. Matarishvan was crouching under the shadow of the bastion. He was clothed in a black dhoti that was longer and tighter than usual. Black boots concealed the rest of his legs. A short black tunic with long sleeves and a black angavastra that concealed his face like a mask ensured that nobody saw his body.

He carried a bow, a quiver of thirty arrows, two swords and five small daggers on his person. A combustible cylinder lay tucked in the folds of his garments. It would, on ignition, shoot up into the sky and produce an eye-catching, vivid, blue explosion that would distract the citizens, giving Bhrigu and Bhairav a chance to escape.

Bhrigu was waiting by the doors. At a signal, he and Bhairav would start beating their drums loudly, at this point, the guards would open the gates, only to wet their dhotis at the sight of the two Aghoris at midnight.

The plan was perfect. All they had to do now was wait.

All the city guards had retreated into a soft slumber. The strong iron gates provided ample defence to the city, housing seven thousand Kalakeyas. At the heart of the city was the Fiery Sky-Lingam Temple of Shiva.

Matarishvan was standing on the wall. There was no activity in the city. It seemed as if everybody was asleep. Matarishvan imitated a barn owl's call, the signal to Bhrigu and Bhairav before jumping right into the city. He had carefully planned the whole operation beforehand, including surveying the city maps to find a spot that would attract zero attention.

He, however, had not expected a pot of metal pans to be kept at the very spot where he would jump. Sixteen clangs were enough to wake up the entire population of that block. Men and women rushed out to see the commotion. The trader to whom the cart belonged was smoking from a paper roll. He was just eight feet away from the cart.

As he went to see the commotion, a bearded man of thirty walked up to him.

"Hey, is that cart yours?"

The merchant nodded.

"Well, keep it down, will ya, ya mother f—"

The merchant punched the man, who bled. The man grabbed his throat, and the merchant kneed him in the crotch. A brawl ensued involving the local neighbourhood, and they all rounded up the merchant, giving Matarishvan a chance to escape.

But he couldn't let the poor merchant die. He fired an arrow that soared with a loud whoosh above a woman's head. The crowd turned to the whistle of the missile as the merchant slipped out and ran.

Matarishvan froze and crouched in the shadows as the city gates were opened, and the two Aghorpanthis walked in.

"Alakh Niranjan!"

"Alakh Niranjan!"

"Bhikhsham Dhehi!" shouted Bhairav, begging for alms. A bowl that suspiciously resembled a cranium was held in his hands.

The two men glared at the crowd in a soul-piercing stare as Matarishvan struggled to hold in his laughter.

"Can we not even be offered a bushel of rice in this godforsaken place? We have marched nonstop from Takshashila to be here. And we aren't even given a place to rest! FIE ON YOU!" shouted Bhairav.

His roar was enough to induce fear in the bravest of men. And this was a city of cowards.

"No, Baba! Please stay!" pleaded the man punched by the merchant.

"THEN GIVE US BREAD AND WATER!"

The man immediately entered his house and came out five minutes later with a flatbread and a mud cup of water, not noticing the black shadow who slid past his ear to climb his roof through the window. He would then run on the nearly same height houses to climb up to reach the closest point to the temple before descending and sneaking into the temple. His fireproof equipment had been tested.

He looked over one last time to see Bhrigu reading the palm of a young girl nearly as old as him.

What a womaniser, he grinned.

83

"Gather around," said Bhrigu gruffly. The people who had woken up by the commotion slowly settled down to see the two ascetics allegedly from the Sapta-Sindhu.

Bhrigu smiled indiscernibly. He could see awe written on the faces of those assembled.

Bhairav was holding a basket that had the Dhaman Virupaksha inside. He was trying to create an aura of mystery around himself and Bhrigu. Ground herbs, strange powders and vials of unknown concoctions were being added repeatedly to the small metal fire facing south in Bhairav.

"O' Kapardin of the matted locks! Bless us with your presence and answer our prayers! Come with all the ghosts, be they from this realm, the previous, or the next. Come to us this night of the Dead Moon and enter the fire. Om Hum Phat Shivaya Swaha!" he said as Bhairav poured in a small ball that turned into serpentine ashes with a lot of grey smoke.

Bhrigu decided to take the act to the next level. He pulled out a paper packet from his bag. A dried and cut mushroom was haphazardly rolled into the paper. It was a hallucinogenic that produced non-lethal seizures at will. Bhairav had worked with the fungus before, but it was Bhrigu's first time. He had clear instructions for only using half of the given amount.

He broke it into two and threw the larger piece ceremonially and with a great pomp. He then ate the other with the chant of 'Om'.

Within seconds, his body reacted, and he began to shake violently. His eyes rolled upwards, and his limbs moved on their own accord. Or so it seemed. His limbs were actually still under his control, but they were shaky. His hand went to his bun, and he ripped away the Rudraksha beads. His other arm pointed to a man in the audience of this show of supernatural power.

Matarishvan turned to look at the man who had just fallen victim to him. Working in a bloodless manner and not killing even a single one of the guards around the temple area.

The last guard turned his back to him and was fast asleep, unaware of how his mates had been knocked out. Matarishvan performed the operation in the same way he had until now.

Placing a solid and fast-acting sedative-coated rag over the guard's nose, Matarishvan grasped his muzzle tightly. A faint moan was heard before the guard passed out. Matarishvan smiled at the success of his mission. Only one task was left now. Matarishvan walked with a new spring in his step towards the Temple of Shiva.

"AAARGH!" rasped Bhrigu as the assembled people retreated a few feet in fear.

The sight of his pupilless eyes on an ash-covered white body shaking like mad and matted locks unbound at midnight in the middle of nowhere would have given most a heart attack.

Aghori. He who is beyond terrifying.

"I…I see…THEFT OF THE FLAMING LINGAM!" Bhrigu growled in the same raspy voice in which he had groaned.

"Let me get Lord Shukracharya," muttered a man as he ran away in panic.

Bhrigu shook with laughter. His beard and moustache covered the smile on his lips, making him shake even more violently.

"Behold! The spirits have possessed my disciple. He is the oracle!" roared Bhairav.

The final stage of the mission was nearing. The eternal flame lay in sight. Just ten feet away was the prize. However, there was a catch. The flame was spread among a crater twenty feet deep and four hundred feet in area. It was nearly impossible to reach the bottom. Nearly.

Matarishvan had come prepared. He threw a pail of water into the flames. Partially doused, the flames took some time but restarted again with the same vigour. He needed more water.

Just as he was thinking of possible solutions to kill the flames, an uppercut delivered by a man built like a bull landed on his chin. Taken by surprise and with his nose and chin bleeding, Matarishvan pulled out a sword from his robes. Stabilising himself, he unsheathed the blade and held the sword in front of him in a typical warrior stance.

The opponent was no one but the assistant to the Lord Shukracharya himself, Arbuda.

Doing justice to his name, which literally meant "mountain", Arbuda had a strict daily schedule which included combat practice and spiritual exercises for fourteen hours a day.

Dressed in a short, red dhoti tied tight at the waist and a black leather vest with matching sandals, Arbuda was a picture of an Asura male beauty. A clean-shaven face and muscular physique, added to his inheritance, were enough for ladies to go crazy for him.

The smile lines around his eyes showed a good sense of humour. Right now, however, they were blazing with the same fury the meteorite behind him was burning.

"No one messes with the Lord," he growled menacingly.

"Try me," said Matarishvan, jumping into the duel.

84

Like all his predecessors, the current Shukracharya, too, had lost all his older identities when he was elected to the post of Shukracharya. He was a little less than eighty-six and had only one eye. His false eyeball had been fashioned from deodar wood, acacia gum and gold leaf.

He stooped over a stick with a very prominent hump on his back. He had a pockmarked face, the gift of cowpox from childhood. Long wispy whiskers that drooped under his jaw could not be differentiated from snowy sideburns that hung from his ears. He had a knobbly knee-shaped head. His ribs protruded from around his lung area and were mainly covered by a rough and prickly blanket that doubled as a cloak, a hooded robe, a shelter and a shawl.

Along with the blanket, his only other possessions were a staff, a kaupinyam and a pair of worn-out sandals because of the vow of ritual poverty the Shukracharya was subject to.

He lived in a chilly cave that leaked during the rains and was quite claustrophobic, again, as per the vows. He had a husky voice, the result of rigorous meditation on icy winter mornings.

A servant walked into the cave, visibly distressed by the changes in temperature and surroundings.

"My Lord, two Aghoris have come. They are fortune-telling and say that they sense danger to the Lord."

The Shukracharya raised an eyebrow, his curiosity piqued. He nodded and followed him.

85

"Oh, just sit down for a while," scolded Shachi.

Jayant wanted to play, but it was time for Sandhya-Vandanam, the evening prayers. Jayanti had already closed her eyes and folded her hands into a namaste before a Deepak. Shachi tried to grab Jayant, but he ducked swiftly and ran away.

Shachi tried to get up, but a pair of arms grabbed Jayant by the waist and held him up.

"And just where do you think you're going, young man?"

It was Vashishth. He had changed completely over the past decade. Battle scars had been replaced by sandal paste. Rudraksha beads adorned what was once covered by diamonds. His beard and hair had grown. Though still black, his hair gave him a withered look, like he was old.

"Oh, come on, Bhratashree!" protested Jayant.

Vashishth chuckled heartily.

"Dear prince, do you know why we invoke the gods thrice daily?" asked the Son of Mitra.

"No," he answered as Vashishth put him down.

"We invoke the gods so that they may protect us. They give us rains, the harvests, the cattle. The streams run because of them; the sun rises because of them. We win wars because they aid us. But nothing in this world is free. We all must pay.

If a fruit seller gives you fruits, you repay him with money. A servant works for you, and you give her money. This is the law and everything is done according to this. Now tell me, what do we, small and insignificant beings, give the gods for this?"

He smiled as Jayant racked his brains.

"We…uh…we offer them ghrita?" he asked timidly.

"Precisely. We give them nourishment. But, more importantly, we give them respect. It is this respect which compels them to help us. And the butter we tediously made that strengthens them to fight our battles."

"I understand, Bhratashree," he said, running off to the worship place.

Vashishth smiled as Indra mouthed 'Thanks.' Vashishth smiled weakly. He had some plans of his own. However, they could wait till the completion of the Sandhya-Vandan ceremony. A few minutes later, the priests finished the prayers with the Prayer for Peace.

Asato ma sadgamaya.
Tamaso ma jyotirgamaya.
Mrityor ma amritam gamaya.
Om shantih, shantih, shantih.
[*Guide us from untruth to reality;*
From darkness to the light;
From death to immortality.
May peace prevail.]

Vashishth closed his eyes in prayer and prayed for guidance.

May the gods be with me.

86

Shukracharya eyed the Aghoris with suspicion. They seemed like frauds.

"No, we're not frauds. And neither are we random guessing, Lord...Maghaabhav," said Bhairav with a grin.

The Shukracharya was dumbfounded. The name seemed very old. It reminded him of his early days, with a loving mother, warm bed, and hearth before he took up his destiny. Before, he was the Shukracharya; his birth name was Maghaabhav.

Bhairav's ability to read minds was a well-guarded secret. Only initiated senior Tantrics knew the secret. Spiritually, it was linked to the Agya chakra, associated with prophecy, visions and going back in time and was located between the brows. Scientifically...?

Proof of Tantric identity had been obtained. Now, for the central part.

"What do you want?" he asked blandly.

"A loaf of bread and a pot of water would suffice for us, Lord. The question is, why are *you* here?" said Bhrigu, emphasising the second-last word.

"What was the theft you were talking about, oh Noble Sadhus?" he calmly asked.

Bhrigu merely smiled and pulled out another piece of the mushroom.

87

"Uncle, I need to talk to you," said Vashishth.

Indra's private office was lacquered gold. He was out in the stables to check on his horses. News had just arrived from Mohenjo-Daro. Pashupati wrote that it was time to bring the war to its final conclusion. Vritra had to be killed. He was already working on Divyastras to launch an attack on Tripura and Kalibangan.

"Yes, Vashishth," sighed an extremely exhausted and thoroughly bored Indra.

"Uncle, I know this is not a good time, but I must tell you something. Chief Vrishakapi has offered me the position of Agastya. The current Agastya shall examine my physical strength, Brahminical learning and general knowledge. I have spent my life learning combat training and learning the scriptures. I really want to try for the position. May I please have your permission to travel with the Vaanars to Southern Aryavarta?"

Indra sighed and then smiled sadly.

"I am going to miss you."

"I'll still come and visit," he promised.

Indra stared hard and made a decision.

"All right. You have the Royal Permission. But what about your father?"

"He, erm..."

"He doesn't agree, does he?" asked Indra.

Vashishth nodded, lips pursed as Indra smiled.

At that moment, Ribhu and his brothers entered.

"Good Morning, my Lord," greeted the brothers.

"Good morning. How is the work on the Ashwins' chariots going on?"

Indra had ordered the craftsmen brothers and Tvashtri to work on two chariots with in-built weapons. But, since Tvashtri was a fugitive, the three brothers had to work overtime in the absence of Tvashtri's brilliant mind.

"Finished and tested, my Lord," came the energetic reply from the sweaty Vaja.

"Good," Indra patted Ribhu on the shoulder and approached the workshops.

88

Matarishvan ducked to avoid the near-death experience with Arbuda's spear. The light spear could be used both as a handheld weapon and as a javelin. It was built in typical Asura fashion: a bamboo handle with a bronze tip and a counterweight that could be used as a club at the back end.

Matarishvan swung his mighty broadsword at the shaft and sliced it into two. Before he could plan his next move, however, his foot was trapped in his dhoti and-

SLAM!

He fell on the floor. Jaws bleeding, he rolled to the side, not giving Arbuda the pleasure of killing him. He would not go down without a final battle. He tore off the extra length of the dhoti while Arbuda, a disciplined, polite and idealistic warrior, waited.

The job done, the two continued to fight like wild oxen. Matarishvan pushed his hobnailed war boot into Arbuda's chest, but it was caught in mid-air by the deranged warrior, who easily held him up in the air and rolled on the ground, ending up on top.

This was the chance. From a distance, it may have looked as if Arbuda had the Marut under his control. But, behind him, Matarishvan extracted his dagger from the sash, camouflaged by the black scabbard, and in one swift slice,

Arbuda's entrails were on the ground. With mustering up all the energy he could, Matarishvan pushed off the mountain-like dying form of Arbuda on the temple floor he had tried his hardest to save.

Matarishvan was moved by the courage of Arbuda, who, even in his dying hours, was trying to reach for his sword. He decided to end the job once and for all.

"Farewell, my brother," he whispered before shooting an arrow through his head.

Deeply saddened at the loss of one of the finest Asura warriors, he sat down to contemplate his actions.

A great warrior. Killed. All because of him. Or was it him? He was merely the instrument performed to do the deed. Who was the real conspirator?

Was it Indra who had ordered him to carry out the mission?

Or was it Dyaus and the older Devendras spreading venom against the Asuras?

Or was it the Asuras themselves, bringing on the hatred of all clans upon themselves?

Never a firm believer in an all-powerful, all-good, pervading God, Matarishvan could, at best, be described as agnostic.

No. The real culprit behind the loss of jewels, such as Arbuda and countless others like him, was the bias of the human mind. Us and them. Sex, caste, clan, tribe, race, nationality, religion, ethnicity. These ideas were exploited by leaders to lead their people in the direction that would lead them to power. The people, like sheep, followed these leaders, thinking that they would lead the flock to greener grass when leading them to a hole. The only solution was unity.

For too long, the Sapta-Sindhu remained divided. It was now time to set up a unified rule—the Rule of the Aryas.

Glorious is the human mind, for all these thoughts occurred to him in less time than it took Arbuda to sputter his last cough of blood before experiencing the sweet release of death.

89

"Om Hum Phat Shivaya Swaha!" chanted Bhairav for the one-hundred and eighth- and final- time. The ceremony was complete. Bhrigu offered half the mushroom to the gods and took the rest.

The seizures grabbed hold of him again as the Shukracharya watched with fascination. Exorcism had been something highly revered in the Asura culture. These experiences of going into trances were considered healing, oracular and divine.

The pupilless eyes stared at the crowd, looking around, searching when they fell on the Shukracharya.

"YOU!" he rasped.

"I sense that... men are going to be killed tonight. Men of HONOUR! A THIEF. IN BLACK. The sky-lingam...g-g-g-gone! RED ARROWS!"

The revelation dumbfounded the assembled people. A theft of an unextinguishable flame? How? And who?

The Shukracharya merely stared at the men.

"You don't believe us?" sneered Bhairav.

"I must confess, I do not fully understand the meaning of your cryptic verses."

Bhrigu was dying to tell the plan but bit his tongue. Hard.

"You will know," he said cryptically.

The corpse of Arbuda had been carefully dragged outside the temple and covered with Matarishvan's own shawl as the shroud. He looked at the heroic face of the dead warrior, spreadeagled before him. He deserved better. A good life, a great house, a loving wife, children. Even the thought of killing such a noble soul was saddening.

Teary-eyed, Matarishvan laid the corpse to rest at a strategic point outside the Holy Temple Premises so that ravens would not attack the corpse.

He then resumed the job of dousing the meteorite. A small but deep pond had been constructed inside the temple gardens, from where he fetched pails of water and doused out the fire before the last remaining substance inside the meteorite that would cause it to spark ignited.

He then gently picked up the meteorite and was surprised by its slight weight. A few years ago, the substance inside would have oozed out of its pores. However, only a little bit of it was left at the centre bottom of the stone.

Matarishvan ripped off his angavastra, wrapped the meteorite into it in the shape of a bundle, and used his baldric to suspend it. He climbed over the temple roof and exited the same way he had entered. The guards were still knocked out.

Good.

He rushed down the same way that he had used to come. Dawn would break in less than an hour. He had very little time. Bhrigu had to be signalled.

The red rocket zoomed over the wall of the city, reaching high up into the heavens and exploded into a shower of red sparks. The city's inhabitants were scared and speechless as they saw the prophecy of the two Aghoris coming through with a "miracle from the gods."

"HAR HAR SHAMBHU!" roared Bhairav and Bhrigu.

Quietly getting up, the men reached for the exit as the men were busy. The Shukracharya noticed this.

"STOP THOSE TWO! I'LL CHECK ON THE TEMPLE!" he roared.

Two guards apprehended the men as The Shukracharya rushed off to the temple.

"Isn't your wife's name Suvisi?" said Bhairav slyly, using his telepathic skills.

"Wha- How…?"

"You want us to curse your fort?" he inquired.

"N-N-N-Noo!"

"Then let us go," he ordered.

The soldier stared in anticipation at the other man, whose face was just as pale as theirs.

"But, Lord Shukra—"

His sentence was cut short by a poisoned dart that flew with the speed of swift as it lodged itself into his neck, followed by another in seconds.

"Bloody good job, Matarishvan!" whispered Bhrigu as the two men ran off.

Outside the city gates, Matarishvan was waiting with a horse-driven merchant cart hidden from view. In it were pails of water, towels, fresh clothes of merchants and jewellery. The buckets were quickly poured to remove the bone ash, and the towels were used to wipe. Both donned fresh garments and pretended to have reached just now at the city walls.

Mission successful.

90

The dungeons of Mohenjo-Daro were infamous in the Sapta-Sindhu. Built thirty feet underground, the rooms were claustrophobic and suffocating even though each cell was twelve by twelve feet. Luxurious compared to other prisons, each cell housed at least three inmates, blankets, one bed, a table, parchment, quills, ink, and a hole that doubled as a latrine. The toilet stank, though. Other than that, the inmates received clean garments and a lot of space. It was here that Tvashtri was housed.

Tvashtri had been immediately and silently arrested as soon as he arrived at the Fort of Manu. He silently cursed the fates in the jail where he had been accommodated. An empty cell was provided to him till such time was decided when Indra would interrogate him. He began chanting the names of the Lord in the back of his mind. Two hours went away in prayer when Indra entered.

The inhabitants of Kotidwija were sprawled on their knees, crying. A prophecy stated that if the fiery sky-lingam were to be moved from its place, the inhabitants would become casteless Mlecchas. That was why the temple had been built after snatching away peasants' land. Mitra and Varuna had just arrived at the city gates, and the wails could be even heard outside the city walls.'

Idiotic bastards, he smiled.

He rode the horse into the city square, the centre of the sorrow. The Shukracharya glared at the tanned Deva rider with the battle scars.

Mitra and Varuna had decided to don traditional Asura colours, red dhotis and white angavastras, leaving their right shoulders bare to allow ease of movement.

"Citizens of Kotidwija, your Shukracharya is a fraud," roared Varuna with emphasis on the last word.

"Guar—," ordered Shukracharya.

"NO!" interrupted Mitra, the Slayer of the Bull.

"You have now become a casteless barbarian, 'ex-' Shukracharya. So kindly refrain from interrupting."

Mitra was thoroughly enjoying himself.

"But, but…" the Shukracharya protested.

"No buts. If you want to agree, listen up. Being a casteless Mleccha is one of the worst fates a man can bring upon himself. We, Devas, are offering you a chance to become us. To become civilised. To become Aryas. For too long, the Asuras have been denied equal human rights. Mistreatment by the Deva classes in the ancient past is responsible for all this.

We are going to change this now. The question is, are you going to join us? Do you want the chance to have a good life? Think of your children. Nursing hatred towards the Devas is alright. But if it is reciprocated because of your actions, how would you like that? We both worship Lord Shiva. Would Lord Shiva have approved of taking poor peasants' property?"

The Shukracharya glared even more menacingly, then rolled his eyes at the orator. He had heard about the Deva 'Arya' propaganda. This stunt could not be pulled with the Kot Diji asuras, one of the most racially 'pure' races of the original Asura tribes from Persia.

However, the people of the city seemed mesmerised by the saviour.

Mitra decided to drive the point home.

"ILLEGAL PROPERTY HAS BEEN SEIZED IN THE TEMPLE, OWNED BY THE LORD SHUKRACHARYA HIMSELF!"

A collective gasp escaped the mouths of those assembled, and all heads turned to the leader.

"Lies!" he declared, though his palms had begun to sweat, and his stomach tingled. His guts felt like lead, and his heart leapt to his throat. He felt the tingle in his perineum, and the urge to urinate overtook him.

Varuna simply threw down the bag in his arms on the floor. Nivatakavacha coins rolled out by the hundreds into the sand of the square. The people were shocked by the betrayal of the Asura leader. Their leader betrayed them and sold them like prostitutes to the Nivatakavachas.

"LYNCH HIM!"

Within minutes, no more Shukracharya.

"We pledge our loyalties to the mighty Ahuras Mitra and Varuna!" roared the town crier.

Win-Win.

91

Disturbing news had just come. The mole had been arrested. Vritra had begun to suspect that Tvashtri was working for the Angiras. But, news of his discovery of being discovered as the Kalakeya informant cleared all doubts.

But, what secrets would he reveal into enemy hands? Vritra pondered this question as a chill travelled up his spine. He racked his brain to remember what he had admitted to Tvashtri.

He had told him of his personal biases and racial ideas and was convinced that nothing important was known by the Angira mole. Vritra now allowed himself to relax and focussed on the more pressing task at hand for which he had come to Tripura.

He slipped his feet into his royal gold and velvet slippers and walked to the largest room of the Swarna, or gold Citadel, home to Danu, Mother of the Dragon.

Vritra knocked thrice on the door. Danu opened the door and bade him enter.

"Good morning, mother," he greeted.

"Good morning, my son," she replied.

"Did you have your breakfast?" he enquired as his gaze fell on the platter of untouched eggs, bread and rice. He sighed with exasperation. Danu had recently been initiated by a

Guru into a spiritual soul-cleansing programme. She would have to give up all material pleasures for forty-one days and abstain from sex, alcohol, meat, unnecessary activities and royal finery.

"I'm sorry. I forgot," he said, picking up the platter.

Vritra tried to talk his mother out of it, for it was a Deva custom. But Dany merely replied-

"Truth is one. Wise men refer to it in different ways."

92

Indra walked into the dungeon, mace in hand. He sat on the low table arranged for him next to Tvashtri's bed. Tvashtri rose up to greet his liege, the Lord of the Devas, the Greatest Devendra, Lord Indra.

The show of mock servility and humility angered Indra to the extent that he raised the mace high in the air.

A heavy weapon of twenty-five pounds, its blunt spiked head and front-concentrated weight added to the impact. It could crush open a man's skull on impact. Just as he was about to attack, a roar was heard.

"NO, MY LORD!"

Hiranyastupa was rushing to Chief Deva like a crazed bull. Indra dropped the mace and annoyed at the distraction, he snorted at Chief Angira.

"What is it, Lord Hiranyastupa?"

"My Lord, he's innocent," he panted.

"Innocent? This bastard has been found sending letters to his 'lover' back in Kalibangan," said Indra sardonically, referring to Vritra.

"My Lord, I can explain," quipped Tvashtri.

"You watch your mouth. You made the Vajra to gain my trust. The Indrastra, too, was a manipulative plot. If you have any respect, however fake, for me, you shall shut your pie-hole NOW!" he growled menacingly.

"Continue," he said turning to Hiranyastupa.

"KUTSA!" barked Hiranyastupa.

The assistant entered the dungeon. It seemed as if he was just standing outside.

"Show His Majesty the letters," he ordered.

Kutsa extracted palm-leaf papers from his satchel and showed them to Indra. Indra rolled his eyes and began to read. The parchment was addressed to Shambara and described the Deva battle plans.

Indra was almost about to say if this was a joke, but his eyes saw the drawing of the army formation, neatly labelled as infantry and cavalry. But, these tactics were never used in Lakshmandurg and were, in fact, the complete opposites of the tactics used. This only meant one thing.

So he was trying to weaken the enemy and was working for me only. But wait...

What if he was against me and Vangrida? If he supports just Vritra...

"No."

"Your Highness, these too," added Kutsa as Indra read on.

These letters were addressed to all Asura Citadels's military leaders on the Sindhu's Western banks. And all of them were wrong.

"But, but..."

"Forgive me, Your Highness. I had to keep the guise of a spy. I am loyal to Guru Brihaspati's mission. Lord Dyaus' mission. It is my Karma to save my motherland. You only quoted Lord Ram. What was it you said? That mother and motherland are greater than heaven? Well, it doesn't seem like that, considering your actions. Holing up in your fort while the inhabitants of the Seven Rivers languish in agony," said Tvashtri, not controlling the venom in his voice and the rising anger that bubbled within.

Indra sighed and dropped to his knees.

"I apologise, my friend. I thought wrong of you. You were plotting the downfall of the Asuras. Why didn't you explain earlier?"

Tvashtri began to weep.

93

The War Council discussed the attack on Tripura inside the Rudra's private audience chamber. Scientists had already finished work on the Divyastra that would be used. The weapon would work similarly to the Agneyastra, but instead of the saltpetre-charcoal-brimstone mixture, it would use a rather explosive form of the Soma paste. Not only would it be unexpected, but Soma paste was known to be one of the most flammable substances that burned with a blaze that reached the heavens, challenging even the waters that would be used to douse it. But the central part was the explosion that could make mountains fall down.

All preparations done, Pashupati had to now only wait for Indra's permission, which would hopefully come by afternoon once Tvashtri was interrogated thoroughly.

"Anything else?" asked the Rudra.

"No? Then please excuse me," he said taking off his crown.

The men stood up in respect for the representative of Lord Shiva. The Rudra acknowledged them with a nod and walked out where Ambika, Shachi and Vashishth were waiting.

"Where is your uncle?" he enquired.

"Still in the dungeons," answered Shachi.

"My family..." began Tvashtri but stopped due to the lump in his throat.

Indra offered him a glass of water, which Tvashtri accepted gratefully. He took a few sips, rinsed his dry mouth and began narrating his story.

"My parents were killed by the Kalakeyas when I was young. I wanted revenge. I was just an average thirteen-year-old, hot-headed teen. So, I joined Lord Rudra's army. This was the time when the Bhutaganas were revolting for their autonomous territories. The violence could not let me live. So, I decided to plot their downfall by pretending to be loyal to them. Over time, I became a double agent. I gave false information on the Bhutaganas as well as the Angiras. However, unimportant real information had to be revealed as they would have suspected me had all their plans failed. My Guru and yours, Lord Brihaspati, instructed me to keep up the guise. I swore on Lord Agni to rid the Sapta-Sindhu of the Kalakeya menace. But how? That's when my mentor died. But, almost when I thought all hope was lost, it seemed as if my Guru was giving me a chance by dying. That was when I met you! The King of the Devas. The Kalakeyas' greatest enemy. So, I plotted the Asuras' downfall."

He couldn't finish further as he began to cry a full burst.

Indra knew what would follow and put his hand on his shoulders, holding him into a tight embrace.

"I'm sorry for doubting you, Tvashtri. Forgive me," said Indra, genuinely moved by the man's plight.

Happiness doubles when you share it, but sorrow halves.

Tarakaksh was staring proudly outside the walls of Gold. Tripura was built in a spiral shape that looked like three concentric circles from a distance. Built on the Northern Banks of the Sindhu, Tripura was one of the best-defended cities of the Kalakeya Empire. The Gold Citadel was in the centre and the best-defended.

Since the city was built as an effective flood control management, dam and a wall to invaders, and not as a metropolis, it only housed soldiers, servants, slaves and a few ministers. Vritra had come to check on the city's security measures and house new immigrants from the south— Asuras in hiding.

The city was now home to new Asura peasants who would farm for the population. A few knew how to work with farm tools and were given polearms. A few were sold as prostitutes.

The Citadel Gold was home to senior Army Officials and was directly under Tarakaksh. Silver was home to mid-ranking soldiers and the army brothel controlled by Kamalaksh. The last, Iron, was defended by the lower soldiers and under Vidyunmali.

The three brothers all had different ambitions and interests. While Tarakaksh preferred an all-Asura united Empire, Kamalaksh wanted peace and an all-clan confederacy promoting peace. Vidyunmali, however, wanted only the Kalakeya supremacy across all the lands.

Vritra walked into the room.

"Tarakaksh, my friend," announced Vritra as he sat on the low sofa.

"My Lord, I didn't—"

"I'm your friend," he smiled.

"Of course," he smiled.

"Well, it's time. I must leave for the capital. You take care. Don't let the bastards grind you down," he smiled, punching him on the shoulder.

Tarakaksh smiled. Then, he went down on one knee, banged a fist on his breast, and bowed in the military salute.

Vritra acknowledged him with a nod, took his sword, adjusted his angavastra and left.

Tarakaksh stood up and resumed the search for visual defects in the fort walls. None.

The only way of destroying the city was…

But that's impossible! After all, who owns a Divyastra at this age?

94

Jayanti, Jayant, Indra, Shachi, Mitra, Urvashi and Varuna were bidding farewell to Vashishth and Vrishakapi, who were leaving for Southern Aryavarta, sailing down the Sindhu to reach the sea and finally reaching the Vindhyachal mountains. Indra had thoughtfully waited till Mitra returned to tell him of Vashishth's decision.

Mitra and Urvashi were teary-eyed as they saw their son, born to be a warrior, leaving to become a rishi. But, it was a rare honour to be an Agastya. Unlike other Brahminical posts, being an Agastya did not require any sort of promotion from post to post. Anyone with the skills could apply, provided they knew stick-fighting, the Vedas and Tamil. The legacy of the greatest Brahmin, Lord Parashuram, was continued here.

"Hey, I promise I'll visit soon! We'll establish relations with the Angiras," he said as Hiranyastupa smiled.

"Of course, once this war ends, we will all live in complete harmony. Lord Devendra, what plans do you have?"

"All right. Listen up. I just had a dream last night when Lord Brahma himself appeared in my dream. He guided me and gave me many ideas. The first was the abolition of all tribes. Arya supremacy could only be achieved if all tribes were unified in one large group like it was before the Kurukshetra war. Even Matarishvan suggested it indirectly—

the second is an exile of the sectarian Asuras. I believe there shall be some sectarian Kalakeyas left after the war. They would need to be ousted or kept in shame. The title I prefer is the Dasyus, a tribe of Dasas or servants. The sheer humiliation would make them regret their decisions and force them to join the tribes. Thirdly, he said a tribe must be sent to Mesopotamia to reform the locals. These would live close to the Nivatakavachas. Not only would they aid us in spying, but they would also reform the leftover Asuras. Lastly, he added that the lost system of the Saptarishi or Seven Sages is reintroduced. They would safeguard the Vedic wisdom. Saying this, the Lord Creator gave me a vision of all the past Brahmas and disappeared from my dream, and I had a final glimpse of Father."

"Wow! That is seriously going to work. But what about the Bhutaganas? And the Agastya's disciples?" asked Vashishth.

"I have already discussed it with Bhairav and Pashupati. They would leave the Sapta-Sindhu and settle around Kailash. They would make their own territories and hopefully spread the message of peace. As for the Agastya's disciples, they can't be categorised as a tribe so that they can continue their existence. Almost all the Saptarishis would be from the Prajapati or the Angira clan since not many other Brahmin tribes are left."

"My Lord, sorry to interrupt, but the Vaanars met a rishi in Persia. He claims to be of Aryavarta origin, and he is the last Brahmin outside Aryavarta. He is well-versed in the scripture, and his ancestors, too, were Saptarishis," said Vrishakapi.

"What is his name?" asked Indra curiously.

"His name is Atri; he is just forty years old!"

"Very well. I shall surely meet him after you come back."

He cried for five hours till no more tears were left. After all, losing a mother is the greatest sorrow even the gods cry on. Vritra had just received news of the brutal attack on the city of Tripura. Corpses of just fifty-four of the many thousand-strong population had been sent to cemeteries. The extraction of just fifty-four corpses pointed to the weapon's ferocity and the archer's unerring aim, the Rudra himself. All this happened when Vritra was three hours away from the city. The attack was done using the dreaded Vaishnavastra.

Named after Lord Vishnu, who was, ironically, "The Preserver," it used Soma and a mixture of chemicals that could decimate entire army segments. The assault was done on the middle of the artificial hillock, which crashed in the middle of the city at a time when every inhabitant was present in the square of Gold.

"Who-…?" croaked Vritra.

"We suspect the involvement of the Devendra," answered Shushna, maintaining a respectful distance from his liege.

Vritra gestured with his eyes to Shushna.

"You want a battle with him?"

"A duel. Just me and him."

"But what if you lose, Your Highness? I mean, the empire? The Kalakeyas? Would you just let the Devas win? I'm not saying you'll lose, but…"

He was stopped silent by Vritra's glare.

"Just you?"

"A small duel. Two on my side. Two on that bastard's."

It was surprising how hoarse and thick grief could make a voice so mellifluous that a cuckoo could be ashamed. Now, no one was left to hear the songs left unsung. The song that Vritra had written for Danu fell out of the pocket and left to crumble into the sands.

"Indra! Indra!"

Pashupati ran into the gardens in front of the audience chamber. Indra and Shachi were holding hands and walking.

"LORD DEVENDRA!"

Indra turned back.

"Vritra has agreed to a duel. Just two people!"

Indra was elated. But he knew that he would have to ask the main questions first.

"But the public?"

"Are mostly Suryavanshis and the Chandravanshi tribes. They think the Asuras have supernatural powers that make them control the nation. But the Gods are coming! The drought would be over, for the God of Rains and Thunder, Lord Indra, is here!" said Pashupati, tears of joy welling up in his eyes.

"Oh, by the way! Congratulations on subduing Tripura."

"All is due to the graces of Lord Shiva and all the Rudras," he said, clutching his Rudraksh pendant.

It was time—the Final War.

95

It was Indra's first visit to Kalibangan, the black fort or the Fort of Death. After the Asuras' war with Lord Vaaman the Aditya, the Daityas were exiled from the Sapta-Sindhu, and the Brahmadurg fort was the Devas'.

However, after the Kurukshetra war, the Kalakeyas captured Brahmadurg and renamed it the Fort of Death. It was in this hotbed of Asuras that Indra had been called for a duel.

As the sun set over the battlefield, Indra rearranged his angavastra, passing it over his left shoulder and tying a knot over his right waist. Sunset was nearing.

Vritra entered. For now, he truly did justice to his name, 'Firstborn of the Dragons.' Dressed in a scaly breastplate with spikes coming out, his black onyx pendant had been embedded in the centre of his breastplate. Dressed in a black dhoti and wearing a black angavastra, he resembled a grey thundercloud. It seemed he had an ensemble of close-combat weapons. His hand held a spear while a sword hung from his belt. His armoured tunic contained metal fragments that could be broken off to double as daggers, and his war boots and helmet were extremely painful.

Indra folded his hands into a namaste and bowed his head to the opponent. Vritra did not even acknowledge him.

He had lost far too much. He did not give a damn about the Sapta-Sindhu, the Kalakeyas, the waters, the dam or his ancestors' legacy. He wanted to unite Indra with the Noose of the God of Death. But Shushna insisted that he elect a second to carry on the legacy and even decide on a regent.

However, Vritra merely dismissed his most trusted General with a glare from his bloodshot eyes. The gods would have cowered had they seen the glare of an orphan. A man who had lost everything and wanted to take everything from the one who had taken everything.

To the surprise of the assembled, it would soon rain. However, Vritra remained unmoved. As did Indra.

"Your rules," began Indra.

Vritra did not say anything but merely threw a roll of parchment on the ground. It held the plan to construct an arena. Indra's soldiers would make a semicircle, and Vritra's would complete a round arena. Indra would have the right to choose the weapon of combat, which was odd since it was believed that all of Vritra's weapons would be used like actual soldiers.

Indra obliged and judged Vritra for a second. He seemed well-versed with the bow and arrow, but a bow would be practically useless since the duel would be close quarters. The spear looked extremely heavy for *him* to handle, and so he moved to the sword.

"I CHOOSE THE SWORD!" roared Indra loud and clear over the din of soldiers marching to form the arena.

Vritra threw away all the weapons except his sword.

"I ACCEPT LORD DEVENDRA'S CHALLENGE… OF THE SWORD!" roared Vritra.

Indra wasted no time and drew out his scimitar from his scabbard. He then tightened his white dhoti and threw off the upper garment. The circle around the two men consisted of the Angiras, Adityas, ten or so Bhutaganas and Kalakeya General.

Indra temporarily fell to his knees and began to pray to Lord Vishnu. To his awe, Vritra repeated the same prayer word by word, copying the same tune, intonations and even the lilt.

The demon-king. Worshipping the slayer of demons.

Indra nodded at him, and the duel officially began. Indra dragged his second-in-command, Kutsa—the descendant of Agni— into the arena while Shushna drew out his own scimitar. The four fought like demons. Indra lunged at Shushna while Kutsa deflected Vritra's slices. Though fast, even Kutsa could tell that Vritra was fighting half-heartedly. Suddenly, it began to drizzle.

The opponents changed, though the energy was the same. This time, Kutsa was fighting with a level-headed Shushna. However, the duel was turning fatal for Kutsa. Indra switched opponents and stabbed Shushna in the gut. The move was reciprocated by Vritra, who missed by an inch.

Thanking the gods, Indra continued to fight and threw his sash at Kutsa. It would act as a bandage. Quickly giving the medical care to himself, Kutsa stood up and resumed fighting. Indra parried a thrust from Vritra. In this manner, the fight continued for an hour until the drizzle turned into a downpour.

Shushna lunged forward as his foot was trapped in his dhoti and fell headfirst. Kutsa wasted no time and stabbed him in the back.

"CHEATING," yelled Kalakeya treasurer Anha as he jumped into the battlefield. Vritra yelled.

"NO!"

And to the surprise of those assembled, Vritra himself stabbed Anha in the back. Indra's eyes nearly popped out of his head as he saw the opponent stabbing his own supporter. Vritra trampled over the corpse and resumed fighting, spitting out two bloody teeth.

The duel ensued and continued with a decreased ferocity. Kutsa had sustained even more injuries, and since only one opponent was left, Indra allowed him to leave the fight.

Hiranyastupa lent him his arm and half-carried him out of the arena where the physicians Nasatya and Dasra were waiting. They had gained mastery over the Ayurveda, the Science of Medicine. This very same talent would allow the twins to once again save the life of Lady Vishpala, the future Deva governor.

The fight ensued without Kutsa and slowed down to a halt with the rain. The men and the gods above were all drained of energy. Thus, the fight and the shower.

However, both resumed half an hour later with full gusto. It seemed as if Indra was controlling the rains with the fight. Out of nowhere—

THWACK!

An uppercut reinforced with an iron gauntlet made contact with his jaw as Indra fell to the ground.

96

Nearly half an hour had passed since Indra lost consciousness. Vritra tried to recharge himself, using it to regain control over his body. He had begun to shake uncontrollably from the grief, rage, adrenaline, hatred and sweat.

Indra opened his eyes to see the Bhutagana physicians preparing the Soma paste while just a few feet away, Dhatura tea was boiling. Indra shook his head to remove the mud from his hair. He felt his numb jaw.

Damn!

The Firstborn of the Dragons got up and smiled at the heavens, ecstatic.

Wait…don't Asuras believe in an afterlife below the ground?

An afterlife above in the heavens with the gods was a custom of the Devas.

What the hell is it with this man?

Vritra slowly opened his waist pouch and extracted a small stone idol of Lord Vishnu, holding it in his hands, praying, drawing strength from it.

"THE DEVA HAS REGAINED CONSCIOUSNESS!"

An Asura had just noticed and roared.

"Let him be. The poor lamb is in no condition to fight," smirked Vritra.

Indra gritted his teeth.

"The poor lamb was killed in Tripura. On my orders," he said.

Vritra lost all good sense of judgement and lunged at him, but the Maruts stopped him. As he crashed into their gold breastplates, the Asuras made a defensive circle around Vritra.

"We fight tomorrow, bastard," he hissed.

The fight had been relocated to a nearby hill, this time without the defensive circle. Indra had prepared for the occasion. His earrings glinted in the morning sun in a white tunic and dhoti, with gold armour and white angavastra. A blue sash belted his tunic in place, and his long hair reached his shoulders.

He held another sword today. This sword had clearly been polished just yesterday and held a new gleaming edge. However, its most distinguishing feature was the acid-etched inscription. '*Dyaus.*'

"Like the sword? If I sold it, it would clearly feed the families of a Kalakeya village for the next generations. It's got sapphires and diamonds in it."

Indra was thoroughly enjoying himself with the battlefield banter.

"SHUT UP, DAMMIT!"

"Oh, of course. Well then, see this," he said, showing him the Vajra he had brought.

"I'm going to use it to k—"

His sentence was cut short as Vritra went down on his knees and began praying to Narasimha, the fierce leonine form of Vishnu.

Ugram Veeram Mahavishnum jwalantam sarvatomukham

Nrisimham bheeshanam bhadram mrityormrityum namamyaham

I bow to the aggressive warrior Mahavishnu, whose face shines like fire in all directions,

I bow to Narasimha, the frightening, the auspicious. I bow to the Death of the Goddess of Death.

Indra picked up his sword and allowed Vritra to charge first.

The usual slash, dodge and slice technique followed by a quick jab. Vritra's will, Indra noticed, seemed indomitable today.

Yesterday, he was an enraged boar, attacking and mauling everything and everyone in his path. Today, however, he was applying strategy to his moves. His sword arm glided about effortlessly but thoughtfully like an eagle.

The metal clangs were accompanied by various hooting and cheering noises from the Maruts.

"MARUTAH VIDYUT!" they thundered.

A frustrated Vritra swung the sword like an axe and caught Indra's aquiline nose.

Indra groaned in pain as Vritra sneered. He had nearly succeeded in killing Indra. The Deva King would have perished just a little bit up or down.

Like the scum he was.

Busy in his musings, Vritra did not notice Indra removing his signet ring with his teeth. The ring held in it a spike. Indra held it out, but Vritra grabbed his hand.

"Not yet, King of the Devas," he sneered as he touched his scabbard.

"What was it you said? That I shall be killed by your puny," he said, gazing at the Vajra.

"Thunderbolt? Well, before that, you shall be gutted by my blade. Sweet dreams, buffoon!" he roared as the dagger came out of the scabbard.

Before he could do anything, he felt an arm over his shoulders nudging him. Vritra turned back, only to get a kick in the groin, lose his balance and fall face-first at Indra's feet.

"You really fell for that, you…" chuckled Indra as Vritra hollered in pain.

Indra went to look for the Vajra. As he reached an arm out for it, he saw Vritra trying to regain his balance.

Unmindful of the pain, he picked up his sword and resumed the fight.

The fight resumed with full gusto. Slashes and slices rained down heavily on both the opponents. From up close, it seemed that Indra was on the losing side. He sported a cut eyebrow, sprained left wrist, torn angavastra and scars all over his muscled arms. But, his spirit remained undaunted.

"This is for my motherland," he roared as the sword made contact with Vritra's arm, cutting a vein.

Momentarily glad, Indra's face drained of colour when he realised it was not his sword arm.

Vritra groaned and adjusted the position of the sword in his hand to a more comfortable one, owing to the strain in his fingers. Indra was exasperated.

Why doesn't he die?

It was high time. The Shatterer of Forts chanted a prayer to Lord Agni. He tightened the grip over his sword and threw away the angavastra he had wrapped to avoid the cold. He didn't need it. He was the Warrior God and gods don't feel cold.

"JAI AGNI!"

The Fire God's name steeled his insides with molten magma from the depths of the Earth. A Vengeful Dragon was not enough to stop Indraagni or Indra's Agni. Or Indra and Agni.

With a bull's roar, Indra leapt in the air and extended his sword arm sharply in the direction of the Dragon. The armour cracked open, and the blade punctured his lung and spleen. As blood flowed down his chapped lips, Vritra smiled.

"I…I…I pr…proved you wrong. I die by the sword," he laughed, blood flowing continuously.

"Oh yes, nearly forgot," Indra smirked and picked up the Vajra.

Indra roared as the thunderbolt was plunged into the chest of his greatest adversary, the Dragon of Drought. His body started to shake violently and char. His eyes went glassy, and his breaths became more ragged until they stopped altogether. It seemed as if a heavenly energy was acting through the Vajra and pulling his soul down to the lands of the ancestors. In traditional Asura lore, the afterlife lay beneath the Earth, unlike Deva culture. As Vritra's body charred away completely, Indra fell down on the battlefield, drained of all energy.

For a final moment, he had the vision of Brihaspati and Dyaus smiling at him. Devas, Angiras, Suryavanshis, Chandravanshis, Bhutaganas; everyone cheered for the victory of the King of the Gods.

The Sapta-Sindhu had finally been liberated from all the scourges of humanity. The clouds burst like never before. The gods rejoiced. The Age of the Aryas had finally begun.

EPILOGUE

1800 BCE, near the Saraswati River

"You all know what followed. Lord Indra survived after drinking copious quantities of the Somaras. Three full pots! The dams were almost instantaneously destroyed after the Decree of Liberated Rivers was passed for all of Aryavarta. The Aryas had been united. The Kalakeya supremacists were ousted from society, never to be seen again. The Tribe of Mitrani was created and sent to Mesopotamia. The Devas themselves chose to return to Amaravati as tribes were outlawed. Lord Rudra led his men away to Mount Kailash. The gods blessed the land with prosperity. But obstacles came in between," said the sage.

The Tribe of Mitrani, or as it was known there, Mitanni, was the group mostly composed of the Persian Vaanars and the Asuras willing to mend their ways. They had made Mitra a god and worshipped him as a clan hero. Tales of his conquests spread far and wide, even reaching Rome.

"What obstacles?" asked the son of the Sarpanch.

"The Chandravanshi clans wished to remain divided ninety years after the Slaying of the Dragon. These ten clans created a confederacy which attacked Lord Divodasa's grandson and Leader of the Bharatas, Lord Sudas. Agastya

Maitravaruni and another Saptarishi, The Chief of the Vishwamitras, were at the head of the battle. It was their rivalry which caused it," he finished.

The boys sat in silence, absorbing this piece of information.

"Who are you?" the dark-skinned boy finally asked.

The rishi smiled.

"I am a Saptarishi, the Last of the Angiras," replied the now five-hundred-year-old Hiranyastupa.

GLOSSARY

Aayushman Bhavah- Traditional Indian blessing. 'May you have a long life.'

Aghnya- Those who must not be killed (in the context of cattle and horses).

Aghori- A sect of monks who are feared due to heretical behaviour such as questioning rituals and consuming alcohol and marijuana. They are devotees of Shiva.

Agnihotra- Morning ritual of chanting prayers while burning cow dung and clarified butter in a copper pyramid.

Ahi- Dragon. Also called Azhdaha (old persian).

Ahura- Lord. It was used to refer to Persian nobles who migrated to the Indian subcontinent. Their Indianized name was the Asuras.

Alakh Niranjan- Used to refer to the Almighty. Literally, '(Salutations to) He who is formless and unperceivable'.

Amrit- A drink made of Soma that can make one live beyond his normal lifespan, even centuries.

Anala- Fire.

Angavastra- Upper garment or torso cloth. A stole worn both by men and women.

Aparanta- Modern-day Baluchistan.

Aryavarta- Historical name used to refer to most of the Indian subcontinent.

Ashwamedha Yagna- A fire sacrifice where a horse is ritually sacrificed along with a castrated ram. There were many versions of it, of which one was the Rajasuya, in which a horse was made to run freely over land, and wherever it passed through unhindered, the land would belong by divine authority to the conductor of the sacrifice. Refusal to let the horse pass would officially mean sacrilege and war.

Avatar- Incarnation.

Bhasma- Sacred ashes.

Bhikhsham Dehi- 'Please give me alms'.

Bhikshuk- Beggar.

Bhratashree- Elder brother.

Bhuta- Ghost.

Chakras- Energy vortexes said to exist within the body at specific places, mastery over which makes one attain superhuman abilities. They are associated with various chemicals and hormonal control within the body.

Chakravyuha- Also called Padma Vyuha, this army formation consists of a giant spiral or concentric circles that is a vicious trap of death to the foe.

Chakshu- The Oxus river.

Chandrahaas- Smile of the Moon.

Dhatura- A poisonous plant that has certain medical properties. It is one of the most crucial components of the Soma (see glossary note on Somalata).

Dholavira- Formerly called Dhumravarni due to its smoky grey walls. An important Indus Valley Civilization site.

Dhoti- Traditional Indian garment worn by tying at the waist and passing between the legs, usually kept together with a waistband or tucking inside.

Divyastra- A variety of weapons encompassing weapons like bombs, water cannons, crossbows, and other incendiary projectiles.

Gada- Traditional Indian mace.

Gau-Harana- Cattle raid.

Ghrita- Ghee; clarified butter.

Gunas- Qualities within an individual. They are three in number—Sattva(bliss or right energy), Rajas(action), and Tamas (sloth or inertia).

Indraagni- Indra and Agni. Or, Indra's fire.

Indraya Vijaya- Victory to Indra.

Janeu- A sacred thread suspended from the shoulder to the hip. It indicates that the wearer has mastered the education and is, therefore, eligible for an occupation that doesn't involve menial jobs.

Kalaantak- Destroyer of Death, Epithet of Bhairav.

Kalibangan- Formerly Brahmadurg. Capital of Vritra and the Kalakeyas.

Kamandalu- Ritual water pot carried by priests and sages.

Kaupinyam- Loincloth worn by sages and warriors.

Ketaki- Screw pine; Kewda.

Kot Diji- Formerly called Kotidwija. An important Asura city home to the Asura religious head, Shukracharya.

Kurma Vyuha- Turtle formation, akin to the Hellenic Phalanx or Legionary *testudo.*

Laddoo- Edible ball made from (usually gram) flour that is primarily sweet and eaten as a dessert.

Lakhanjo Daro- Formerly Lakshmandurg. An important Asura citadel home to the Asura Vangrida.

Lingam- A stump placed upon a pedestal. Foreigners consider the Lingam as a mere phallic stump. However, it represents the energy of creation. The stump represents Shiva – the masculine energy – and the pedestal represents Shakti – the feminine energy.

Lothal- An important trade centre of the Indus Valley Civilization.

Lungi- Traditional Indian male nightwear. A sarong tied like a skirt.

Malla-Yuddha- Traditional Indian sport of wrestling and other physical combat.

Mantra- Sacred chant.

Marutah Vidyut- Battle cry of the Maruts. 'The Maruts are Lightning.'

Mausala- Iron club used in Malla-Yuddha.

Mehrgarh- The Fort of the Panis..

Melukkha- Mesopotamian name of India.

Mleccha- Foreigner; barbarian.

Mohenjo-Daro- Formerly Manavdurg. The Fort of the Rudra is named after Lord Manu, the progenitor of Indian Civilization.

Mudra- Gold coin.

Muhurta- Auspicious time period.

Narak- Afterlife of the Asuras. It is also the name of Hell in Deva culture.

Naravrishabha- Bull among Men.

Praanvayu- Literally, 'the air of life'. The ancient Indian name of oxygen.

Rishi- Seer, sage, or enlightened person.

Rudrasya Maryah- The Raudras' battle-cry. 'The Warriors of Rudra'.

Sadhu- Monk or sage.

Sandhya-Vandanam- Evening prayers.

Sanskrit- The language of the Devas, banned under Asura rule, which led to the change in the names of cities, such as Lakshmandurg became Lakhanjo Daro.

Sanyas- Compulsory renunciation of the world accompanied by asceticism practiced by men in Ancient India after the age of seventy-five.

Sapta-Sindhu- The historical region between the Indus River and the Aravalli Hills. Named after the seven rivers that lined it- The Sindhu(Indus), Shatadri(Sutlej), Vipasha(Beas), Sarasvati, Parushni(Ravi), Asikni(Chenab) and Vitasta(Jhelum).

Shanti- Peace.

Shastra Vidya- Warcraft, Ancient Indian combat training focussing on physical strength as well as weaponry.

Somalata- The vine used to make Somaras.

Somaras- It is a drink or paste that can make one cross physical limitations such as tiredness, lack of strength and enhance one's body with infused vigour, speed, and strength. In extremely concentrated or heavy forms (Amrit), it can even increase the drinker's lifespan. It is extremely poisonous in its raw form. That is why it is drunk with a specially treated infusion of Dhatura (thornapple) and mead.

Surkotda- an ancient town in modern-day Gujarat.

Tasmai- The Persian precursor to the modern-day Kheer/ Payasam.

Tilak- Sacred mark or dot worn on the forehead, or less popularly, on the chest, arms, and stomach. They showcase the wearer's devotion to the deity of his choice.

Trimurti- The triple gods, Creator, Preserver and Destroyer.

Tripura- Three citadels built in concentric circles that controlled Vritra's dams.

Udaanvayu- Literally, 'air that floats,' an Ancient Indian name for Hydrogen.

Uparishyena- Ancient name of the Hindu Kush range. Its name means 'One crossed by the Shyena(falcon).' Shyena is also an epithet of Agni, making it the mountain range crossed by Agni.

Vimana- Flying machines.

Vrisha- Bull.

ACKNOWLEDGMENTS

मनोजवं मारुततुल्यवेगं जितेन्द्रियं बुद्धिमतां वरिष्ठ ।
वातात्मजं वानरयूथमुख्यं श्रीरामदूतं शरणं प्रपद्ये ॥

Ever since I was a kid, my best friend, Hanuman Ji, has been my Supreme Guiding Light and my superhero due to whom I was inclined towards mythology. My inclination towards mythology and history made me write this book. I am short of words to thank him for empowering me with his *Bala*, *Buddhi,* and *Vidya*.

Next, I want to thank all the people who have stood by me in writing this book. They are more than what you would think:

First of all, my Daddy, Mr. Satya Prakash Soni, the first person who knew before me that I could write a book ever since I was ten. This book is the product of his constant guidance and support. He tried to make the book better in every aspect, even while posted away from me. An avid reader himself, he has always been there to quench my craving for more and more books.

I want to thank Maa, Dr Somi Soni, my true critic. Her watchful eyes ensured I didn't succumb to the temptation of scrolling memes. Countless cups of chai while writing this book are another reason for being grateful to her. She is the one who always ensures that whatever I do, I put honest efforts into it.

I want to thank my little sister, Pari, for being the first audience of my stories. She nags me to take breaks after finishing three pages, a chapter, or any other time so that I can play or watch TV with her. However, she helped me even in the most minor ways.

I want to thank my *Nanaji* Dr. Loknath Soni and *Nanisa*, Mrs. Santosh Soni. I'm incredibly grateful to my Nanisa, as she planted the seed of mythology in my head. It was due to her that even before I was three, I knew the Hanuman Chalisa, the Ramayana, the Mahabharata, various Puranic stories, and multiple regional stories about the gods. I used to keep her awake all night to keep listening to stories.

I am grateful to my *Baba* and *Amma*, Mr. Babulal Soni and Mrs. Nirmala Soni. Baba's extensive knowledge of metallurgy helped me quite a bit in the book (and passing my Chemistry exams too).

I am grateful to my *Mama* and *Mausi*, Mr. Lokesh Soni and Dr. Romi Soni, for guiding me through multiple aspects., My *Mausi* Romisa needs special mention for having faith in me and encouraging me always.

I am also obliged to my Tauji, Mr. Sanjay Soni, Mr. Suresh Soni and Mr. Shankar Soni. Suresh ji Tauji need special mention for having faith in me and encouraging me always.

I am obliged to my cousins; Shivani Didi, Mayank Bhaiya, Khushi Didi, Anushka, Keshav, Harsh Bhaiya and Siddhi who are my greatest and first friends.

I am grateful to Reverend Father Principal M. Arockiam and my teachers from my school, Saint Xavier's, Jaipur.

To Sindhu Ma'am, Sapna Ma'am, Santosh Ma'am, Jiss Mary Ma'am, Seema Ma'am, Olive Ma'am, Babita Ma'am, Govind Sir, Stephie Ma'am, Aradhana Ma'am, Rama Ma'am, Shabana Ma'am, Sumit Sir, Christine Ma'am; as well as my librarian, Mr. Pratap Lakra who have always been the guiding lights of my knowledge.

To my all-time favourite teacher, the one who got me interested in History and English, Anant Henry Sir.

I want to thank my school friends Tanishq, Shridhar, Ayaan, Aarav, and Raghuvansh for bearing with my mythological ranting.

I am deeply obliged to my publishing team at NuVoice Press for giving me a chance. I am thankful to my favourite author, Kevin Missal Sir, for giving me a chance. I would also like to thank Navya Ma'am, Vini Ma'am, Deepika Ma'am, Tarun Sir from the team, and all the others who helped me. Vini Ma'am was kind enough to guide me through all the meetings, and I'm grateful for that.

Lastly, I would like to thank the King of the Gods, the Shatterer of Forts, the Firstborn of the Gods, the Lord of the Waters, the Saviour of Cows, and the Wielder of the Thunderbolt –Lord Indra. Lord Indra is often revered as the Lord of the human mind, and I could experience his energies when I had random brainwaves and guesses that turned out to be true when I read up on them later.

Thank you everyone!

ABOUT THE AUTHOR

Abhiveer Soni is a young and talented author who belongs to Jaipur. Despite his tender age of 14, he possesses an insatiable appetite for knowledge and a deep passion for literature. He is a student of St. Xavier's School, Jaipur. His interests range from history to Indian, Egyptian and Greek mythology, and religious texts.

Abhiveer's unique perspective and youthful energy shines through in his work, making him a rising star in the literary world.